STUDIES IN THE THOUGHT WORLD

OR

PRACTICAL MIND ART

BY

HENRY WOOD

AUTHOR OF " IDEAL SUGGESTION" " GOD'S IMAGE IN MAN"
" EDWARD BURTON" " THE POLITICAL ECONOMY
OF NATURAL LAW" ETC.

*Great men are they who see that spiritual is stronger than any
material force; that thoughts rule the world.* — EMERSON.

1896

PREFACE.

In response to frequent requests from friendly co-workers and students of truth, these disconnected studies are gathered and presented to the public in book form. A part of the volume consists of lectures and essays which have not before been published, while the others (subjected to some changes) are here reproduced through the courtesy of the publishers of the various magazines in which they originally appeared.[1]

While all the papers are metaphysical, psychological, or evolutionary in character, they are, with one or two exceptions, essentially unitary, and therefore the order in which they are placed is not significant. Like "short stories," each is measurably complete in itself.

The power, quality, and exercise of the human thinking-faculty are attracting unwonted attention and interest, and the potency of concentrated ideals

---

[1] The magazines referred to are *The Metaphysical Magazine*, New York; *The Arena*, Boston; *Universal Truth*, Chicago; *The Christian Metaphysician*, Chicago; *The Journal of Hygiene*, New York; *Health Culture*, New York; and one or two others which have been discontinued.

is increasingly understood and utilized. The priceless value of impersonal truth, and the saving power of optimism, are receiving increased and merited appreciation.

It is not merely a duty, but rather a privilege, for the author of this book to join with many others in urging forward the great cause of the higher life, and of a general human incarnation of the divine quality.

All truth which is above the plane of the intellect should be accepted, not upon external authority, but just in the measure that it receives the full sanction of the inner "Guide," or spiritual intuition of the individual. To aid in and point out the law of the development of this supernal faculty to his readers is the writer's earnest desire and effort.

It may be observed that some basic principles are reiterated in various settings and combinations. This is due to the character of the book, and to the fact that vital truth needs repeated and positive delineation in order that it may become mentally graphic.

BOSTON, 1896.

CONTENTS.

	PAGE
OWNERSHIP THROUGH IDEALISM	9
THE EVOLUTIONARY CLIMB OF MAN	18
A GREAT ART MUSEUM	40
THE VITAL ENERGY AND ITS INCREASE	46
A CORRECTED STANDPOINT IN PSYCHICAL RESEARCH	53
THE DIVINITY OF NATURE	63
THE HYGIENE OF THE CONSCIOUSNESS	82
WHAT IS MAN?	87
OUR RELATIONS TO ENVIRONMENT	100
DIVINITY AND HUMANITY	108
HAS MENTAL HEALING A VALID SCIENTIFIC AND RELIGIOUS BASIS?	113
THE UNITY OF DIVERSITY	148
THE DYNAMICS OF MIND	156
AUTO-SUGGESTION AND CONCENTRATION	170
HUMAN EVOLUTION AND THE "FALL"	180
OMNIPRESENT DIVINITY	197
MENTAL AND PHYSICAL CHEMISTRY IN THE HUMAN ECONOMY	213
THE EDUCATION OF THOUGHT	232
THE NATURE AND USES OF PAIN	238
THE SUB-CONSCIOUS MIND	250
THE PSYCHOLOGY OF CRIME	256
THE SIGNS OF THE TIMES	267

STUDIES IN THE THOUGHT WORLD.

OWNERSHIP THROUGH IDEALISM.

THERE is a universal craving for desirable things; but in many particulars there would be wide variation of opinion as to what is deservedly to be sought. The subjective bias of different individuals is very unlike; and it is this, rather than abstract merit, which determines the quality and intensity of personal demand.

The lack of completeness is a universal feeling; therefore there is a general reaching out for something not yet realized. This longing is vague, and not readily interpreted; consequently its real significance is generally misunderstood. Experience shows that, as one object after another that has been sought is gained, the demand is at once enlarged; so that, contrary to expectation, the feeling of incompleteness, instead of being satisfied, is even more accentuated. Man stretches out his hands, and grasps that which he has craved, but is surprised to find that the hunger within him has moved forward, and far outstripped its former outermost limit. When intelligently comprehended, however, he finds that this divine dissatisfaction is what differentiates him from the beast, and keeps him faced God-ward.

Alexander wept for other worlds to conquer; and this spirit of out-reaching for new accomplishments and greater possessions is a universal experience. One who had attained everything he desired would be rightly accounted either as abnormal or idiotic. There will be a normal feeling of incompleteness in every human being until, in a certain sense, he feels and realizes that all things are his own.

The cravings of humanity begin upon the lowest plane, and not only expand in breadth, but reach continually higher. The infantile demand for simple warmth and nourishment is but the starting-point of desires which are absolutely illimitable in extent and duration. On all the lower planes of consciousness the expectation is general that perfect contentment is to follow the attainment of present low and limited ideals. This acts like a powerful but ever-retreating magnet, which draws men onward, and still onward.

The young man who engages in business says, "When I have accumulated such a sum I shall be content, and anything further will be a superfluity." But before that point is reached the resistless demand has swept on in advance. The artist sets before him a high standard which will fill the measure of his ambition; but, in time, that which was at the summit of his desire is left below in the dim distance. The scientist will solve a great problem, or utilize a new discovery, and then rest contentedly upon his laurels; but, as he moves on, grander views loom up before him, and unseen hands beckon him forward. This universal soul-hunger for complement, or rather possession, is normal and good. It is the divinity in man which gravitates upward.

But wholesome dissatisfaction, like every other normal quality, is capable of perversion; and this mistake is almost universal upon the lower planes of man's nature. This noble quality, which in the evolutionary unfoldment of the past was only reached as he emerged above the level of animalism, is unwittingly turned backward in its action, and centred upon things which are below its own legitimate domain. Alexander's desire to conquer was laudable, but his application of the law was a sadly erroneous one.

Every one may rightly aspire to "own the earth," but not through physical conquest, or by means of legal title-deeds and exclusion. There is a higher and a truer kind of ownership. The realist will exclaim that such an idea is purely imaginative, and has no solid basis. But let us look more deeply. It is true that, in a sense, we often have outward possession or control of things we do not own. But making the closest application of true ownership, let us inquire as to the proper method of taking an inventory of one's assets.

Before passing to the metaphysical definition of ownership, which is by far the most real and intrinsic, it is proper to say that we do not in the least impinge upon the legitimate rights of material ownership in its own domain. This right, as recognized by all organized governments, is to be sacredly observed. To question it would be to introduce anarchy and chaos in the place of law and order. It is indispensable upon its own plane and in its own time, and will rightly remain until outgrown by regular processes of evolutionary advancement.

The millionnaire is the object of much envy because his actual possessions are assumed to be large. But real ownership requires *capacity*. That important factor has been left out of the account. No one can truly own beyond it. A legal title may give outward *control*, but true ownership is deeper. Capacity, or power to contain, cannot be enlarged to order. In reality, one owns that which he can absorb, appropriate, and appreciate, and no more.

Suppose two men together roam through a great conservatory. One has the title-deeds of the same in his pocket, but is quite destitute of all æsthetic feeling and cultivation. To him it is only a piece of "property" representing a sum of money. It is not a conservatory in uses or purpose. He is incapable of its real ownership. Its wealth consists not even in the color, fragrance, and graceful proportion of every plant and flower, but in their intelligent appreciation. Its *value* is contained in the delight which these can awaken in the soul of the beholder. As a conservatory it has no other uses. The companion of the title-holder may be penniless; but, if he have the developed capacity, the riches he beholds are his own. The other may externally manage a conservatory, but he cannot own one. The same is true of the riches of a great library, and of the beauty and quality enshrined in art, architecture, nature, or a landscape. But ownership, in its true sense, is not limited to the æsthetic appreciation of material things, but covers the whole range of moral and spiritual quality and attainment. Even the ideal things in the character of our neighbor, which we have not yet actualized, are ours, through love and appreciation. Every true quality that one desires is his, wherever it be found. We may thus take possession and pay for what we wish, without the formality of legal documents, "signed, sealed, and delivered."

The wealth of the realist and materialist is very meagre, for they are only rich in deficiency and limitation. Riches to them are impossible except through the narrow channel of title-deeds. Instead of entering into possession of the admitted superior qualities of their neighbor, contrast makes them feel poor. To rejoice in another's superior and superb health, wisdom, talent, or beauty, which we are not yet manifesting, is gradually to take possession of them without dispossessing him. Idealism breeds riches because the good, the true, and the beautiful, in their universal aggregate, belong, not merely to the community in general, but to each individual member. Measured by the financial scale, each one becomes a multi-millionnaire, minus the usual care and anxiety.

If the ego be soul, and not matter, it is obvious that all real proprietorship must be mental and spiritual. Of necessity it must be subjective, while the holding of legal titles means only objective regulation. The treasures of the mind and investments in ideals are not subject to decline or bankruptcy, and the market is never glutted. With the enlargement of the capital stock comes the continual growth of the power of acquirement. But those mental powers which through a special training gain an expertness that commands only a commercial value — which comprises nine-tenths of so-called education — are only technical and subordinate. True education is the increase of the richness of the mind for its own sake.

All the accumulated attainments of science, triumphs of art, researches of philosophy, achievements of invention, penetration of logic, music of poetry, grandeur of heroism — even the ecstasy of love, the beauty of virtue, and the very inspiration of the Spirit of Truth — belong, not all to all, but all to each. Emerson, the great idealist and intuitive philosopher of modern times, graphically moulds this grand truth: —

OWNERSHIP THROUGH IDEALISM.

"I am owner of the sphere,
Of the seven stars and the solar year,
Of Cæsar's hand and Plato's brain,
Of Lord Christ's heart and Shakespeare's strain."

Idealism is the vital element in religion. Paul, philosopher as well as apostle, crowned the apex of a pyramid of spiritual wealth with the aphorism, "All things are yours." From Plato down to Emerson, all the great idealists have been capitalists in the profoundest sense.

What a contrast between the puny, material title-deed, which is not only superficial, but exclusive, and the ideal law of acquirement, whereby every one may own everything! Poverty is a condition of soul. This is even true on the material plane. The millionnaire who feels poor *is* poor, and nothing but a mental revolution can make him otherwise. On the other hand, the humblest task and the simplest gift may be transmuted into a pleasure and privilege. The world is full of poor people who are rich, but they are utterly unaware of it. There are boundless deposits of virtue, love, goodness, beauty, health, and happiness waiting for drafts to be made upon them. But the eyes of the world in general are fixed upon deficiency, and they see little else.

The pessimist will ridicule such a philosophy, and tell us to come down to the facts; to get out of the clouds, and stand upon the solid ground. He hugs his own woes, and asks, Is not the earth full of wretchedness and illness, and poverty and oppression? Apparently, yes; but it has all been gratuitously self-created. The seen negative creations have not been made in a moment, and it is not claimed that idealism will at once transform them. True subjective wealth is a growth. But so soon as the *law* of accumulation is grasped, the trend of the world will be rapidly toward universal wealth on every plane. Human vision has been almost entirely filled with outlines of limitation. We must "right about face." Every one can be rich because he can multiply his ideals and *hold* them. As this is done, they press with ever-increasing intensity toward expression, articulation, and actuality.

Every one loves his own ideals. His fancy is not for his actual friend, duty, occupation, book, or profession, but for his ideals of these. He paints them in his own colors, and loves them for the aspect he has thrown around them. Even lovers love not each other, but their own mental pictures. Thus everything real and normal may be clothed with beauty. But our ideals, however fine, cannot exceed the intrinsic actual. Expression to-day may be faulty, but the constructive vision penetrates beneath the outwardly imperfect to the coming manifestation of the Real.

Our aspirations are all too low. The inmost actual will at length have expression. Everything is therefore intrinsically better than it seems, because we have made up our opinions from superficial incompleteness. We can rectify, yes, re-create, the external universe by polishing the subjective lens through which we view it. The highest attainment to be sought is the incapacity to see evil. Contrary to the conventional view, this greatly increases our ability to correct it. To fill ourselves with a knowledge of it, in order to combat it, is like attempting to drive darkness out of a cellar without the aid of light. Thought-space is possession; therefore, to think no evil is simply to have no ownership of it. In proportion as it becomes unfamiliar to consciousness, it is remitted to oblivion.

The mind is the depository of its own riches. Even the beauty of a landscape dwells in the beholder. Idealism is the electric motor, by means of which we may make rapid transit from inharmony to harmony, and from poverty to wealth. We go to the ends of the earth to find riches in climate, air, scenery, art, entertainment, and health, with indifferent success. The divine restlessness is upon us, but we misinterpret it. Our poverty is outwardly apparent. Let us therefore turn within, to the safety-deposit of Mind, and acquaint ourselves with its treasures.

THE EVOLUTIONARY CLIMB OF MAN.

THE eons of the past have been occupied with a struggle to bring forth man. That great effort is still in progress, for he is not yet completed. Generic man, or the human ideal, is, and always was, potentially complete; but in actualized existence and expression he is ever more becoming.

This is an era of remarkable progress and discovery. But the most wonderful of all the new accomplishments is man's discovery of himself. Only through evolutionary interpretation has this been possible. Without such a divining-rod he had no way to measure his own proportions, or to estimate his relations, and therefore had no idea of his size and importance.

The new philosophy has proved to be a universal clew; but, though we may follow it faithfully, we shall never arrive at its end. Only in its light can phenomena be translated, whether organic, inorganic, vegetal, animal, human, intellectual, or spiritual. It is the new mental telescope; and only through its lenses can be discerned the universal trend and specific aim of the cosmic economy. As before noted, its whole end and purpose — that " for which the whole creation groaneth and travaileth " — is the bringing forth of man.

In a very realistic sense, evolution has created a new heaven and a new earth, and, in fact, made all things new. Take all the so-called sciences, and they would not now recognize their likenesses, as faithfully taken two score of years ago. Geology, botany, zoölogy, astronomy, biology, in fact cosmology, which embraces them all, are to us new creations. All the theories, systems, text-books, and authorities extant, that have been formulated without the light of this all-inclusive philosophy, are worthless lumber, warped and decayed. They are as incongruous as the Ptolemaic system of astronomy.

In this special study we are not to take up, technically, the details of material evolution; for these have been ably formulated by modern exponents from Darwin to Drummond, and to do this would require an especial equipment to which we lay no claim. Our purpose is rather to interpret the spirit, trend, and meaning of this great philosophy, as we follow its clew among the higher aspects, and to trace its all-inclusiveness in man.

Lifted from its blind materialism, evolution may be simply defined as the divine method of continuous creation; or, in more specific terms, as God's way of making ideal man — or the man that is finally to be the full expression of himself. To accomplish this grand work taxes the entire cosmic resources.

Evolution is not to be reconciled to the various fragmentary systems, dogmas, and opinions that have been built up into disconnected structures in the human consciousness of the past; but these must all come before its judgment-bar, and receive its righteous verdict. The truth — to just the degree that it is contained in them — will not only be electively made manifest, but put in orderly and connected form. Before tracing, a little in detail, some incidents that have occurred during the interminable human march to the present vantage-ground, we must establish a very radical and significant premise.

Evolution, as conventionally set forth, has been grossly materialistic. It has dealt with mere figures, rather than the numbers which they represent; with sensuous forms, instead of the moulding force which shapes and rules them. The materialism of Darwin still lingers largely with most of the recent exponents of the new philosophy. But though their attention has been almost exclusively centred upon outward forms, — which are only indexes, — yet even such superficiality has been indispensably useful as a stepping-stone to the deeper reality. A knowledge that recognizes progress in beauty, complexity and perfection of form, leads to an understanding of the advancing orderly shaping force, which is thus given outward expression. Visible forms are only symptomatic of the moulding reality that is back of them, the quality of which they are striving to express.

They are the printed characters which tell a great truth. It is admitted that forms are endowed with a quality called life or soul; but this has been regarded as an incidental property resulting from organization. Mere fortuitous combination was thus looked upon as a creator of life. Cause was mistaken for effect. Definitely stated, it is that matter evolves itself, or that it could be both actor and material acted upon. Darwin embodied it in his famous aphorism, "All potency is contained in matter."

Sensuous science has made an effort to eliminate divinity from nature and man, or at least to crowd it back to the most remote protoplasmic energy. Secondary gods have been set up, and labelled "natural selection," "chemical affinity," "inherent energy," and "resident forces," in the attempt to make a great orderly, unitary Intelligence unnecessary. It has virtually assumed that matter grows in and of itself. In its conflict with theology, science has almost out-dogmatized the dogmatists, by teaching a practical though unadmitted atheism.

On the other hand, the ranks of traditional literalism have become exceeding thin, and few remain who still hold that a Deific fiat suddenly created all things from nothing.

There is an impassable gulf between evolution and all special dispensations. Every link in the endless chain of events is firmly attached to the ones which precede and succeed it. If the established order has ever been abruptly broken into from without, upon any plane whatsoever, then evolution is a myth. God reigns in and through orderly law, and is never self-contradictory. When reverently followed, a true evolutionary philosophy leads up to the conclusion that all phenomena are the manifestations of one Infinite Mind.

True evolution, in its essence, is the name of a law of progress, rather than of a series of seen forms. The life, mind, or soul, of whatever grade, is always the cause, and not the result, of organization. The real progression is in the ascending quality of mind or life. Each step is a successive state of internal character, and its visible form is only its sensuous translation.

It is not matter, *per se*, that progresses. The same physical material appears, disappears, and reappears in higher or lower combinations, as the case may be. It is passive clay grasped by the hand of a moulder. The elements which to-day make up the body of a dog or tree may have figured long ago in the material organism of a seer or philosopher. There was no ascent or descent in the material, but only in its user. All progress is in the unseen. Your body is not you, but only your outpicturing index. The seen figure is not the progressive reality, but just the well-fitting clothing which shows the quality and taste of its present owner. The human ego picks up material, and erects it into an animated statue, in perfect correspondence to its interior quality. If he drop the material, and it be utilized by a horse life or mind, it at once assumes the corresponding equine expression in every detail. There is no exception to this rule. In the deepest sense, the real tree is the tree-life, and not the temporary material which it has grasped for outward expression. True, we may study and admire the latter, but it is unprofitable to invert the relation. A piece of marble, or even a clod of earth, has a kind of life. It will be increasingly evident that all true evolution is metaphysical.

In the great cycle of creative development, the Divine life, first involved into the lowest conditions, is at length, through a series of grand steps, gathered, organized, individuated, and evolved into "sons of God," in which form, with ever-growing reciprocal affection, the return is made to the "Father's House."

Realizing now distinctly that progress is located entirely in the quality and complexity of life, mind, and soul, of which the ascending outward forms are only indexes, we emerge from the thick fog of materialism into the clear sunlight of the true, progressive reality. Visible shapes are only the printed text which is to be read and interpreted. We cannot afford longer to mistake mere numerals on the blackboard for the realities of number for which they stand.

It will then be understood that, in noting some of the steps and processes which man in his lower estate has passed over, we are dealing with his unseen but real self, rather than the wayside inns along the road, in which he has been temporarily sheltered. The promise and potency of coming perfected spiritual man was assured from the beginning of the involution of divine energy into the lowest elemental conditions. The protoplasmic quickening that lies at the foundation of all things stands for and is a definite prophecy of man as finally complete in God's image. The Spirit of God, moving upon and involving itself into primal conditions, is the eternal conception and gestation which will continue until archetypal man shall be born into full expression.

What interminable struggles and efforts, and evolutions upon evolutions, all working for "one divine event to which the whole creation moves"! Based upon the prodigality of expenditure, what infinite value must be placed upon man, always bearing in mind that he is soul, and not body!

How such a comprehensive view puts us in universal touch and fellowship with all forms of life! Everything is not only our friend, but our consanguineal relative. Each has been a kind of abiding-place along the great highway over which we have passed.

What a leap upwards was that from the inorganic

to the organic! But the same omnipresent divine life binds the rock into form that thrills through the soul of an archangel. Mollusk, fish, reptile, and mammal — these grand subdivisions, each again many times subdivided, *all* these, form the rounds of the ladder upon which we have been climbing.

The tremendous ascent is a many-graded school, and the supreme lessons to be acquired are self-conscious individuality, and a developed recognition of oneness with our source.

The psychic nature of man was potentially present in the very clods of the valley. Every lesser grade of life made its supreme contribution, and passed it along to the next in order. All in turn have been melted in that vital crucible whose contents is being cast into man.

The road to a spiritual self-consciousness has been hewn through a great forest of expressive forms, each of which has been pushed aside for its more able successor. The clod becomes a vegetable, the vegetable an animal, the animal a man, the man a self-conscious spirit, and the spirit a god. We must ever bear in mind that all this progress is in positive quality of life, and that each of the rising forms is only its outward symbol. It is like a banner which shows the rank of the force which is marching behind it.

All the motives, mysteries, riddles, and potentialities of the universe find their solution and focalized climax in man. The world is, because he is. He is its reason and explanation. All things are concerned in his coming and becoming. Humanity is the universal goal, toward which, from all directions, there is a supreme effort. From the primal cell upward, everything has this tendency, aim, and transcendent purpose. Man is eternally begotten by the one Omnipresent Life, and is forever being born. The fingers of God, who is Spirit, are all through the cosmos, shaping the life or mind of every atom and molecule, and impressing upon it its grand destiny.

Our family kindred reside on every terrace that is stretched between the amœba and Shakespeare, the reptile and Emerson. Each atom and molecule has magnetic polarity, and its polar star is humanity. The tree is coming man not yet loosened from the ground, and the fossil long ago passed on his best contribution and is resting a while. The evolutionary vesture is a robe, woven without seam, from bottom to top, from protoplasm to seraph.

Man is not only poetically, but scientifically, a microcosm. In the profound deeps of his being, in orderly arrangement, are sun, moon, fixed stars, comets, mountains and valleys, trees and flowers, quadrupeds and birds, with all variations and possibilities, terrestrial and celestial. Man is in the universe, and the universe is in him.

The memories and traces of our brutehood still linger with us, and all our friction comes because we lose our equilibrium by lagging behind the normal onward trend. Any man who loses his soul is the man who has not found it. The great command which rings down through the ages is, "Forward!" and our failure to fall into line is responsible for all abnormity.

As suns, with their worlds and satellites, float in the free and fluid ether, so all sensuous matter rests upon its spiritual base. Mind slumbers in the pebble, dreams in the plant, gathers energy in the animal, and awakens to self-conscious discovery in the soul of man. The psyche of the lower form, involved from the One Life and Mind, for the great purpose of education through evolution, at length learns its great lesson, and takes its degree. Adam could name all the animals out of his own past qualitative experiences. Evolution may, therefore, simply be defined as experimental education.

An endless caravan is travelling on the "King's highway," and each section is laboriously toiling up the gradual, spiral ascent. But from the deceptive materialistic standpoint many things seem to fall away, and drop out of the procession. Forms dissolve, shapes disappear, things are said to die, buds and leaves and blossoms wither and fade; but the unseen life, which for a while held them in form, resumes its march in yet sweeter and more noble configurations. Conservation is the universal law, therefore nothing real can be lost.

The animal psyche is tethered to a little circle

of instincts; but the human soul, although on the present plane connected with expressive materiality, mounts aloft and abroad in ever-increasing range. Not until the ever-expanding psyche has reached the human estate can it turn around and look inward upon itself, and discover the engraved pattern of divinity.

To bring human expression up to the full normal standard requires innumerable eons of frictions, polishings, and experiences. All lower conformations are but a stammering prophecy of the becoming ideal. There is a re-birth in every death, so that the conventional demise of one order is far more exactly the advent of the next.

Man is to be the personal expresser of the one Creative Spirit; so that purposeful evolution is a multiplying of self-conscious, divine personalities. The upward spiral stretches from infinite involution to infinite evolution. The God-energy stores itself in the humblest forms; and as the oak is potential in the acorn, so man is wrapped up in every one of them. The process of ripening is orderly on all planes.

When man discovers that God is in his being, he feels an impulse to give him manifested expression. Life is a great gulf-stream, sweeping away from divinity, and bearing everything on its bosom, but only to finally float all back in perfected form to their primal source. During this great cycle, individuation and voluntary God-likeness are developed.

All creation is through thought, or, more exactly, each thought is a creation. Looking back upon the great cosmic economy, at first sight it seems blended, confused, and even chaotic. Evolution takes this seeming complex entanglement in hand, and through an orderly discipline erects its eternal masterpiece, — completed man. But this purposeful outline and ideal is not yet filled out. Man always lived, and moved, and had his being in God, but must needs be created in low form, or distanced from the Deity in consciousness, in order that he might discover his true rank, through the process of working his way back. In reality, he has never been away from the "Father's House," except through his dream in sensuous matter, and material embodiment. "The Word became flesh" in order that flesh might finally become "The Word."

Having thus briefly traced the outlines of the great evolutionary cycle, let us turn for a little to consider a few of the laws or methods through which we may accelerate the process of our own unfoldment. On all the inferior planes, progress comes from a pushing from behind, and is accompanied by friction. Lessons are difficult, acquirement slow, and seeming mal-adjustments many. The wheels of progress groan and creak upon their axles, often hardly moving, or even appearing to move backwards.

But when the plateau of spiritual understanding

is finally reached, man, through the knowledge of law, begins to aid powerfully in his own advancement. He learns the uses of ideals, and places them in front, where, like great magnets, they draw him onward. He finds the highway smoothed and made easy before him, and glides along without the jarring and grinding of his former movement. He becomes a conscious creator, which only means that the divinity within him has come to self-recognition. *Unconscious* creation is always slow and labored. It grinds its way among obstacles, as a glacier presses forward into a valley, crowded by the huge mass from behind. This continual friction in the human economy results from ignorance of law, and its fruits are dis-order, dis-ease, mal-adjustment, arrested development, decay, and premature material disembodiment.

We have spoken of matter as mere passive material which is grasped by various grades of life for formal expression. We have also said that there was no dead material, and that everything possesses some quality of life. How can this seeming inconsistency be reconciled? Live material is sufficiently passive for all purposes of utilization. All life is positive in degree; but it is law that, of whatever grade it may be, it moulds and uses those forms which are less positive than itself. Therefore man's physical organism is composed of myriads of inferior organisms, and his mind of an aggregation of the subordinate mentality of the past. We have not only left behind us on the evolutionary highway all the lower and simpler qualities of existence, but we also have brought them with us, and have them in us.

Man cannot go out beyond himself, for the universe is contained within the circumference of his being. In him potentially exist celestial harmonies and hellish flames, heavenly ecstasies and demoniacal orgies. He has the equipment to play saint or sinner, devil or angel.

We may now consider more definitely how man, having arrived at that plane of the conscious possession of creative power resident in his own volition, can supplement the universal trend in perfecting his own expression. He has come to the point where he understands himself, because he observes the forces that evolution has employed in bringing him up to his present altitude. What may be called the law of uses is a vital principle, and its scope is universal. If we neglect to exercise any talent, power, or quality, it soon falls away from us. Nature, in the widest sense, always casts away all her useless material. She refuses to nourish all drones, until they finally die from inanition. If, however, we wish to eliminate the brutish forces that still lurk within us, we need not destroy their energy, but turn it into a higher channel. In every past step of biological progress, organs which have served their purpose drop away; but it must not be forgotten that they are always supplanted by a more worthy successor. But the legitimate use of a talent actually feeds it.

The eternal climb through the ages has come from an ever-present inherent craving, not only for more, but for higher and better and richer. Demand always brings supply, and it is entirely adequate. Potentiality is limitless; and it invites you to help yourself, and take what you want. But if our wants are not centred upon that which is superior to present attainment, their supply only puts us back, to again learn a lesson more dearly than before, which really belongs to the past. There is a universal desire for happiness; and happiness means harmony, or rather harmonious development.

If an arm be not used, it at length becomes paralyzed; but the lack of use is more deeply located than might at first appear. It is in the neglect of the thought, or a disuse of the will-power, which moves the arm. The paralysis is, therefore, really in the mind, or in its lack of self-assertion. The arm has only expressed the condition that is back of it.

All advancement is in intelligent, qualitative thought; and visible progress of form is such thought, in uses poured through embodiment. It is only mind-art that produces material, artistic expression. The outer form is necessary on its own plane, but the inner and immaterial entity must insist upon a faithful correspondence. The body, therefore, must not be denied, but affirmed. Denial of it is suicidal. The degree of perfection in embodiment corresponds to the positiveness of the life, mind, and spirit which permeate it. All flesh is malleable stuff, and belief shapes it to its own specifications. Belief should, therefore, be enlarged, enriched and perfected. Its precise view of objective things is of secondary importance, but its estimate of itself is of transcendent import. The mind is a self-begetting and self-creating unitary force. It is always drawing its own proportions, and taking its own photograph. To exercise a true mind-art in securing harmony of outline is the divinest employment of the law of uses.

Thought-energy is the primal and universal force, and executive will is the king of all motors. It rallies all less positive forms of life into conformity, and quickens every normal function into wholesome activity.

The upward ascent of man gives him an ever-increasing breadth of outlook. Like some bold Alpine climber, he rises above the lowland fogs and mists into the clear azure; and at length the lesser peaks which he has left behind, and which before seemed formidable, melt into insignificance. Day by day the mysteries of nature are resolved, and the murky medium into which he has been vainly peering becomes transparent. The subtle mechanism of the universe is laid bare, and the fine links which connect it with mind are felt and interpreted. Unfoldment being a universal law, the upward mental and spiritual climb of man is immutably guaranteed.

One of the present great distinctive features of the evolutionary rise is, that racial solidarity is coming to the surface of human consciousness. Mankind is like a great tree, the branches and leaves of which — all springing from one root, and nourished by the same sap — spread themselves forth that they may feel the glow of the sunlight.

While there is but One Life, it appears broken into a vast number of disjointed fragments, but without any loss of individual responsibility; each belongs to the race, which, as a whole, would be incomplete without him. Every one seems, to himself, finited and separate; but in reality each life is like a bit of color in one great mosaic design.

The coming ideal is universal brotherhood. This will not be attained by any external panacea, or legislative expedient, but by a fusing and unifying of heart and desire.

One may think that he thinks for himself, but more exactly he is borne along by great thought-currents in which he is immersed. He is not much more independent of his fellows than is a piece of driftwood of its surroundings in the rapids of a mighty river.

It is true that the great thought movements have

their individual articulators, who seem to be leaders; but they are really the visible signs of some general trend. They are not commanders, but focalized embodiments of forces which are back of them.

The great sea of human mentality rises and falls, ebbs and flows, in huge tides, and not in detached drops. A perfect network of invisible ties binds men into a great solidarity. The thunder of the rhythmic march of the great mass drowns the light footfalls of the few who would mark an independent time.

Does this in any degree discourage individual advancement? Rather the reverse; for, in a deep sense, every man is the race. The very foremost pioneer, in his progress toward the human ideal, represents a universal possibility and coming goal. We are thinking, willing, loving, and doing, not merely, or even mainly, for ourselves, but for mankind. Even the seeming hard law of "the survival of the fittest," when fully interpreted, is found to be beneficent; for the fittest are really channels and models for the less fit. Every special individual attainment not only brings up the general average, but is a standing object-lesson and ideal. Service, as a fundamental law, must reach down from the higher to the lower. But, in the past, human personality has been so earnestly engaged in working out its own salvation, that it has overlooked its organic relations.

"Save your own soul" has been the reiterated injunction; but the most ideal salvation is the merging of the own soul in devotion to the general soul. There is not only a common divine incarnation, but, in a very real sense, we live in each other.

We wrestle with "principalities and powers," and that in the presence of a great cloud of interested witnesses. The disciplinary and educational experiences of one are those of all, and the victories of each are a general inspiration. "No man liveth to himself, and no man dieth to himself." The ever-widening circles of a human divine consciousness, as a thought-quality, go out in waves to refresh the whole family of man.

Every human brother, as he pushes on in advance, gives an upward impulse along the innumerable lines which radiate from him as a centre. He is a saviour who breaks captive's chains, opens prison-doors, and proclaims freedom. The great evolutionary campaign will not be ended until every member of the race has been transformed into a "son of God."

When the basic law of race-solidarity is generally perceived, it will be a privilege for the strong to carry the burdens of the weak, until they finally disappear. The race being an organism, its unity is only rendered complete from the unlike office of its various members.

Many of the conventions of our modern civilization are the results of arrested development. We wander from the great smooth normal highway, into the seductive by-paths of cold intellectualism, material formalism, superficial education, and of a realism falsely called artistic. Artificial walls and barriers are built up between souls, and the living fountains of human love and sympathy are sealed or frozen over. Society, through an unwritten and unspoken legislation, imposes arbitrary laws which are based upon selfishness and worldly policy. Each soul wears a polished armor, which, though unseen, is as cold and impenetrable as steel. Only a thorough recognition of the law of love and oneness can ever melt it away. Human society still feels itself to be a mass of disconnected units, having adverse interests, and each still inquires, "Am I my brother's keeper?"

The law of ministry is not only an ethical obligation, but a scientific means of progress. If all were just equally advanced in evolutionary unfoldment, there would be little opportunity for mutual aid and bestowment. Like the diverse members of an organism, each is necessary to the completeness of the whole. But the crust of our worldly wise conventions must be broken up before we can be free to cling in graceful embrace to neighboring souls.

The higher life is not a mere refinement of what is lower, but an awakening — the glow of the divine image within, which is restlessly waiting for free expressive conformation.

But, as before indicated, all frictions, arrested developments, and even mistaken by-paths, have an educational use. Many lessons, to be thoroughly learned, have to be ground in by disciplinary experiences. It seems unaccountable, but it is a fact, that we generally refuse to learn them in any easier manner.

But such correction, and even punishment, — if we choose to call it so, — is really the teacher of racial solidarity. Human relationship is so intimate and reciprocal, that the lawful and innocent suffer with and for those who are lawless and guilty. Vicarious experiences are not confined to one historic expression, but are universal. Such a commingling — though having a superficial appearance of injustice — breaks the boundary walls of the smaller or personal interest, and by its educative revelations brings into view the Larger Unit. The righteous man suffers with the malefactor, and the latter finds succor in the former; and such is universal experience, and such is law. What a paradox! Has not Law made a mistake? No; only our selfish concern makes her seem unreasonable.

If each suffered solely for his personal transgressions, it might teach him prudence on his own account; but now he finds that he helps to pay a general penalty, and that his interest is woven into the very warp and woof of the whole social fabric. There is no other true and supreme interpretation of law. The transcendent lesson to come into human consciousness is, that the *summum bonum* of the smaller unit can only come enclosed within that of the greater. In the deepest analysis there are no possible adverse interests. Those which seem so are only superficial.

The Established Order is not only for and within man, but it is man. No true social science, political economy, ethical system, or coherent religion can be formulated except upon the basis that man is One. An individual soul might as easily be split in twain, as for a part of the racial soul to be saved, and the rest lost. The law of the conservation of soul-energy is as exact and scientific as is its correspondence on the lower plane. Only error and falsity are sloughed off, while all that is true is indestructible. The supremest work of every man lies in his efforts towards the unfoldment of the general soul in which he is comprehended.

We are gradually approaching the Kingdom of the Real, where all men will feel themselves to be one because they are united in God. Humanity ultimates in the Universal Soul, but without any loss of individuality. There is to be an eternal welding of Fatherhood, sonship, and brotherhood. When this state of consciousness is reached, one universal heart-throb will send the vital current of love and unity coursing through the veins of the remotest member.

A GREAT ART MUSEUM.

MAN is mind. He is an unconscious artist, dwelling in the midst of an endless variety of mental pictures. His time is spent in photographing things around him, and in taking impressions from his thoughts and ideas. The great palaces of art, like the Louvre of Paris and the Uffizi and Pitti of Florence, contain a vast number of galleries and corridors where pictures are hung, high and low; but mental art museums are incomparably more extensive and varied. Finished productions from the hand of the most gifted artist are crude and clumsy of execution when compared with the expert delineations of the imaging faculty of the mind — or rather the man.

What a profusion of immaterial works of art, each surrounded with a carved frame of accessories, each with its high light and low light, sunshine and shadow, and all without any sensuous limitations of length, breadth, or space! Thought is the artist; and it is ever executing real but intangible masterpieces with marvellous facility, giving them all its own peculiar tone and finish, and putting its initials upon them. The ego is the owner, custodian, and sole visitor of its galleries, and is always inspecting its art treasures. These are arranged not only on walls, but are packed away in drawers and compartments for prospective use and reference. But in the twinkling of an eye they can be snatched from their seclusion, placed upon an easel, and lighted up with the sunshine of consciousness. New and original designs for the gallery are constantly being outlined, and filled in with color from the native pigments of imaginations and ideals.

The bewildering array of statues in the halls of the Vatican are not comparable in number and perfection to those hosts of living figures that are ranged in the mental corridors. The busy chisel of the unknown sculptor is ever carving animated statues with exquisite pose and finish, and placing them on pedestals where they are convenient for inspection. These are more enduring than marble because they are formed of a *less perishable* material.

The power of thought as a creator has, until recently, received but slight recognition. It has generally been left to care for itself, to roam at its own sweet will, and to sketch at random. It is true that pictures, unbidden, and sometimes very unwelcome, flash themselves upon the living canvas; but there is nothing to compel us to sit and gaze upon them. They soon dissolve if we turn our eyes towards a higher order of art, or stand face to face with the ideal.

The pure and matchless art of the devout monk

Fra Angelico, by which he was able to depict angelic beings with such beauty and delicacy, was the natural outcome of the spiritual atmosphere of love, joy, and harmony in which his consciousness made its abode. He created the world in which he lived, and the base and false had no place in it.

Tennyson thus sings of an inner ideal art:—

> "O all things fair to sate my various eyes!
> O shapes and hues that please me well!
> O silent faces of the Great and Wise,
> My gods, with whom I dwell."

Any one of a thousand acquaintances can only be recognized and identified by comparison with the portrait of him that is already hanging — perhaps for years — in our invisible gallery. A single mental photograph lying undisturbed for twenty years in the "dark room" is suddenly called for, snatched from its hiding-place, and found to exactly correspond with its material duplicate now presented. But personal portraits form but an infinitesimal part of the varied innumerable shapes that make up the resources of the immaterial palace of art. Still beyond the domain of the more sensuous pictures of external objects there is a deeper skill and vision which produces and dwells among moral and spiritual entities. Its keen, penetrating glance is focused upon delineations of love, faith, purity, and goodness, and include glimpses of the Great Reality. "The pure in heart shall see God."

A GREAT ART MUSEUM. 43

Thought, the imaging artist, is perpetually designing and executing new works, and consciousness is untiring in the inspection of its stock on hand. It, however, lingers longest in those corridors where its loves and affinities are most profusely represented.

Down in its gloomy basement there is a great illusive network of hidden passage-ways, the walls of which are covered with unseemly outlines, and the arches and ceilings with indistinct and smoky frescoes of hate, envy, lust, and selfishness. The bats and vampires of evil imaginings are flying to and fro, and the atmosphere is clammy and morbid. But for a delusive earthy gravitation the mistaken consciousness would not explore these deeps, much less remain to inspect and analyze their contents. There are also in this basement more inviting doors, opening into corridors that seem flooded with rosy light, which shines out at the entrances, making their figures appear artistically beautiful. But upon a closer and an internal inspection, the forms are found to be hollow, repulsive, and to crumble at the touch. Every niche is occupied by some suggestive and fascinating statue which enchants the senses and invites intimacy, but a more thorough acquaintance reveals its deceitful and ugly features.

Other unlooked-for portals admit the unsuspecting consciousness into dark, damp corridors hung with pictures of disease and deformity. Pale and ghastly forms abound, and lenses of fear and expectation are ingeniously placed so as to multiply them. The Pale Horse, with his Rider, occupies the most conspicuous position in the collection. On every hand are found brushes, pigments, and fresh canvases for the production of new and more complicated abnormal designs. The very atmosphere is offensive and charged with miasma and mortality.

O Consciousness! grasp the hand of Idealism, and leave this false and unwholesome domain, and ascend to the sunlit apartments of the Real. Behold what harmonious and delightful scenes, done in enduring colors, here meet the gaze! Every statue is erect and graceful in pose, pure in form, and divine in expression. The realm of shadows has been exchanged for the kingdom of realities. To linger here is to gain the artistic ability to execute more and better, and thus beautiful forms are multiplied.

Mount still higher to the Supreme Ideal. In the most lofty sanctum to which the Consciousness can aspire, stands a figure of typical perfection. Love, purity, peace, and beauty are eloquent in every feature, and from it is radiated a celestial halo, soft and harmonious. Thought, the artist, has carved this statue during the highest flights of its inspiration, and left it upon its pedestal as its supreme effort. No other sculptor has aided in its execution, for each subjective artist designs and executes only its own. This is the Christ within, and no external power can remove or disturb it.

Linger in this Presence, O Consciousness, for it will at length transform thee into its own glorious likeness. Come up often from the lower and baser domains; sit in the silence, and be *at home* in the divine auditorium of your nature.

THE VITAL ENERGY AND ITS INCREASE.

EVERY living thing has an inherent potential force which may be said to be the mainspring of its organism. This energy is so strong and constant that it not only holds in check all corruptive and disintegrative tendencies, but it has positive and formative power. Under normal conditions it is a veritable "dynamo" which transmutes and moulds material into new and characteristic form and expression. This force we call life, but a better definition would be mind.

When mind has laid hold of matter, and erected it into a symmetrical animated statue, so long as this mastery continues, we say, "Here is life." When this mysterious union ceases, or, in other words, the mind lets go of its material, we call the change "death." The matter which has been released from the grasp of the living entity disintegrates. But nothing has died. There has been no forfeiture except simply that of a peculiar form of expression. The essence or mind has discontinued its use of that particular material which it for a time employed for out-picturing or objective manifestation.

Every living form is an external index of some kind of mind. In every detail it is a result, and never a cause. For instance, the tiger-mind picks up material, and moulds it in every particular to express exactly the mental propensities and characteristics of that animal. Feline cunning, ferocity, strength, and adaptation to environment are all mental qualities. Body is passive material, being only acted upon.

The life (or even here we may say the mind) of a beech-tree gathers up matter and erects it into a shape, but never makes a mistake regarding the exact form of visible expression. The grain of the wood, bark, every branch, twig, and leaf, all articulate *beech*, and nothing else.

The human mind, or life, erects its own animate form with exactitude, though the identical material may have been used for other grades of mind a hundred times before.

We have thus concisely stated a few basic principles of being, to note by contrast the baselessness of prevailing materialism. Without intending to be materialistic, we unconsciously become so, judging as we do by outside appearances. We fall into the superficial current, and gauge everything by sensuous measurement. Careful reflection will show us that we are always dealing with surface symptoms and effects, and fail to get down to the depths of primary causation. We drop into the error of regarding mind only as a quality of body, while in reality the latter is merely its instrument. The mind is the substance or entity, as is a number, rather than the figure or character by which it is represented.

Any other philosophy of being than the above makes man a mere bundle of animated matter, and presents him as dependent for his very existence upon a fortuitous concourse of organized material. If mind be only a function or attenuated quality of co-operative dust, what becomes of it when disorganization takes place? We will do well to dismiss such a deadly pessimistic philosophy.

Have not therapeutics, philosophy, science, and theology all together become materialistic? Man regards himself as a material being. He practically thinks of himself as body. This state of consciousness degrades and puts him upon the plane of innumerable limitations.

Metaphysical science and experience show that so far as one holds as a positive principle that *he* is *soul*, and that it is normal for him to rule his physical instrument, thus far he gains a growing power and control over it. This thought, firmly and continuously held, so moulds and influences the body, that at length it not only renders a useful and harmonious ministry to its lord and master, but also becomes increasingly impervious to disorder and inharmony. This doctrine exactly fits the constitution of man. It is in accord with law in its deepest and broadest interpretation.

Bearing these points in mind, let us inquire what are life and health? Life is that condition in which the real man, ego, or mind, rules and also receives normal tribute from his sensuous organism. Health is that state of relationship when there is no insurrection or obstacle, and peace and co-operation prevail. The man rules his household, and receives rightful service and respect. The divine established order is recognized and complied with.

Illness is that condition in which the rule of mind is enfeebled, or when the grasp of the ego is weakening upon its legitimate kingdom; and death is the entire loss of its executive hold and authority.

To successfully reign in his lawful domain, man needs added vitality, and a felt connection with the universal exuberant Energy. He must regard himself as a conduit, and be in constant receipt of supplies from the great supersensuous Fountain of Life.

It is not the passive clay which needs manipulation, but the ruler who must have added executive authority. His weakened grasp must be tightened; and this is not possible by visible food only, for "man shall not live by bread alone." If the ego firmly assert its positive supremacy as a matter of divine right, its demands will be complied with. The "divine right of kings" is as nothing in comparison.

We patch the body from the outside, hoping thereby to make it mentally tenable a little longer. *But it is built from within.* From the inner to the outer is the universal established order.

Mental causation is always primary, but it is too deep for sensuous observation. The draft may *occasion* a cold, but the *cause* is more subtle, — susceptibility.

Every one has long been aware that fear, grief, sin, anxiety, pessimism, and all their train, pull down bodily tissue; but we have unwittingly failed to observe that their positive opposites would surely build it up. But this is logical and reasonable. Harmony, joy, optimism, idealism, love, and courage will surely invigorate. Under the now well-understood law of auto-suggestion and thought-concentration, each mental condition can be positively cultivated and made dominant in the consciousness. It is possible to entirely change the mental habit. A daily exercise of immaterial gymnastics, involving systematic thought concentration, is as practicable as any system of muscular and physical development.

What, then, is the remedy for mental or physical infelicity? Change the subjective standpoint. Reconstruct the consciousness. It may not be done in a moment, for all growth is gradual. But the same pains and persistence that we give to a thousand things of far less importance will work a wonderful change in a short time.

We must consciously enter into our possession, and

claim that we are living souls rather than poor, weak, material creatures. Dwell not in mere physical sensation, upon the animal plane, but in an affirmed and cultivated conscious superiority over conditions, until they fall into line and serve us. Enthrone the real ego, which is spirit, created in the image of the Infinite, and utilize something of that divine potency which has been hidden by ages of self-imposed limitation.

But man, having lost his spiritual self-consciousness, mistakes the handful of dust which he has for a while utilized, for himself. By immutable law he manifests and outpictures this concept which he has held and carelessly actualized. So long as he regards himself as a poor, weak, material creature he will fill the measure of his own outline.

"As a man thinketh in his heart so is he." This is not a mere moral or religious platitude, but a scientific statement. It has been said that "a man is the architect of his own fortune;" but this is more true of mind and body than of worldly place and possessions. The creative power of thought is his divine instrument; but he has not learned its use, and so, as has till recently been the case with electrical energy, its force has been squandered, or, even worse, turned in the wrong direction.

Man searches the objective world over for balms, specifics, and panaceas, and experiments with every known external thing, but fails to interpret the nearest and grandest of all things, — his own constitution. He goes abroad for congenial environment, sunny skies, and favoring climates, but fails to get away from his own perverted thoughts concerning himself. He must learn that through ideals he may displace his spectres. By compliance with this great law he may transform seeming adverse conditions. The "Philosopher's Stone" is within his own being. Through the spiritual alembic of his inner nature he may rightfully call for all things to pay him tribute.

A CORRECTED STANDPOINT IN PSYCHICAL RESEARCH.

We are so accustomed to deal directly and almost solely with the objective, that any attempt to readjust our own end of a line of relationship is unconventional, and by many is regarded as irregular, if not unscientific. The great obstacle to the apprehension of truth is not so much in its complexity or occultism, as in the lack of perception that is consequent upon predisposition, bias, authority, and even upon what is often regarded as learning itself.

Not long since a prominent clergyman, whose dogmatism is most pronounced, preached from the text, "Whosoever shall not receive the kingdom of God as a little child, shall in no wise enter therein." But to whom is it more difficult to become childlike, in the reception of truth, than to one whose creed is positive, whose opinions are fixed, and to whom "revelation" is fully completed?

The dogmatism of theology is often paralleled by that of so-called science. To venture beyond the conventional limits of the regular materialistic schools, or to question their traditional methods, subjects one to the charge of being eccentic, and often requires more courage than is needed for a new departure in the realm of theology. In other words, the scientist is often quite as punctilious regarding "orthodoxy" in his own domain as is the dogmatic theologian in his. To approach a subject in such a way as to get a view of its true outline often necessitates the brushing away of much subjective rubbish which unconsciously hides the very object sought. True insight is often gained only at the expense of some preliminary *un*learning. With a proposed effort to search for truth is often linked a strong, even though unconscious, desire for evidence to confirm existing opinions. Authority, traditionalism, and unsymmetrical education are often, one or all, fatal to the openness, plasticity, and intuitive transparency which are indispensable to the discovery and reception of things which are deep and veritable. Prevailing systems of education are scholastic rather than educive. That conventional cramming of unrelated objective facts, termed learning, is the rival, if not the enemy, of a delicate and impartial inner perception through which truth comes into the consciousness. The excessive intellectuality of the age, being entirely objective, has dulled and obscured the keenness of the intuitional faculty, which normally is of higher rank.

Coming to a more specific application of these principles as related to psychical investigation, it is evident that a higher point of view would greatly

A CORRECTED STANDPOINT.

facilitate progress. Disregarding, therefore, not only the traditions of the regular materialistic scientists, but also the methods of many other earnest explorers, well intentioned, but almost wholly objective, we propose a brief introspective study among foundation principles.

If we look at mind and spirit from the plane of materiality, we find ourselves in a valley which lacks breadth of outlook. While practically regarding our*selves* as bodies, we naturally begin to speculate whether or not it be scientifically possible for that airy, intangible something called mind to act, live, and be conscious when its physical "basis" is laid aside. Our prevailing objective materialism gives us the feeling — from careless habits of thought — that mind depends upon material organism rather than the reverse. Does body build life and mind, or do they build body for the purpose of outward and correspondential expression? Manifestly the latter. The former would logically end in pure materialism; but it is remarkable that thousands are practically thorough materialists without being aware of the fact.

The real man (ego) is mind, soul, spirit. He *is* soul, and *has* a body. Nearly all will agree to this proposition in the abstract; but so soon as they begin to reason in any direction, they unconsciously abandon their premises, and practically regard themselves as *material* beings. With daily consciousness centred exclusively upon the sensuous and objective, it becomes almost impossible, from force of habit, to maintain a correct standpoint and perspective. How greatly it would simplify all psychological research to squarely hold the position, not that we *have* souls, but that we *are* souls — yes, spirits — *now*, as much as we ever shall be. The physical organism is no part of *us*, but it is expression made visible — nothing more and no less. To be sure, it is educational; for it is in accordance with law that soul must have an experience in matter. But it is important that we educate our thought to regard the body only as an instrument belonging to the man, entirely secondary and resultant.

If soul be only a function or exercise of body, as conventional "science" and *materia medica* have practically assumed, then immortality is illogical; for when a thing perishes, its functions, which depend upon it, perish also.

The body, being but a sensuous form or plane of expression for the real man, bears a similar relation to him to that of his clothing. He is not merely its tenant, however, but its architect and builder. Its construction is from within through the force of mind, conscious and unconscious. Thought — mind in action — is creative. It is the universal motor and the fountain of primary causation. There are molecular changes in the "gray matter" of the brain, but they are the material correspondence or result, and not the cause of thinking.

A CORRECTED STANDPOINT.

While many physical processes take place involuntarily, or below the surface of consciousness, they are nevertheless all directed by mind. But a small part of mentality is upon the plane of consciousness. The key to the interpretation of a large part of the phenomena of hypnotism, psychology, and mental therapeutics is found in a proper discrimination between the objective and subjective mind. The latter, which is so responsive to suggestion, and which so directly moulds and directs all bodily activity, till quite recently has hardly been considered.

The atom, or theoretical unit of matter, has not yet been discovered, and therefore is, to this day, only an intellectual abstraction; but although scalpel has never touched it, nor microscope revealed it, we need not question its existence. But whatever it be, its use is to objectively express different grades, qualities, and operations of life, or organized mind. The same material is picked up and used in one form after another, to temporarily manifest the special peculiarities of the life that is then using it, in exact correspondence. At length disintegration follows, and leaves it free to be again seized upon as before. It logically follows that life, or organized mind, is more deeply *real* than matter, and the immaterial than the material. The former is true *substance*, the latter more properly shadow. Taking the evidence of the real, intuitional self or ego against the objective or sensuous self, we con-

clude that reality, permanency, and solidity are
terms which can only be properly applied to mind
and spirit. As in the case of the apparent revolution of the sun around the earth, sensuous appearances are misleading. The world for so long a time
has had its consciousness filled with forms and expressions, that it has almost become incapable of
beholding the immaterial. Any faculty long unused
gradually decays.

The evolutionary philosophy, from the changed
standpoint, becomes simplified and intelligible. If
matter be passive, and the same material be re-
peatedly used in integration and disintegration, it
is plain that the progression is only in the advancing qualities of organized life and mind; and these
successively embody and express themselves in suit-
able and corresponding shapes. After full expression, each of these external correspondences dissolves,
and the plastic material of which it was composed
is again utilized and built up anew. The matter
which composes a human form to-day may be found,
a few decades hence, built up into plant or animal
form, to manifest the particular quality of life which
then possesses it. It is over and over again erected
into living statues, sometimes of higher and again of
lower plane, demonstrating that evolution is entirely
and solely of the organized immaterial life, and not
of its passive material.

Look which way we may, we are brought back to

A CORRECTED STANDPOINT. 59

the fact that, in any deep and exhaustive sense, *reality* can only be predicated of the unseen and immaterial. Iron, steel, and gold are unreal and unsubstantial, as compared with mind and spirit. Material science all through the ages has been dealing with shadows, and it has not only insisted that they were solids, but has denied solidity to everything else. The recent conclusion of science that the universal interplanetary ether has a solidity vastly greater than steel, is one of many significant hints of the coming emphasis that will everywhere be placed upon unseen entities and forces. If life and mind are the supreme realities, they, instead of matter, constitute the *substance* of things, sensuous testimony to the contrary notwithstanding. The oak-tree life picks up plastic material, but it never makes the mistake of erecting it into a birch or maple expression. The same principles hold good on the animal and human planes. The law is uniform and universal. We find that all sequential expression is uniformly exact to the most minute detail, not only in species, but in quality, amongst its own class.

Advance a step farther, and note that outward expression, assuredly when the human plane is reached, is not a mechanical, but an intelligent manifestation. The embodiment is an index to the quality of past thought; for thought is a secondary creator. That thought sequences are slow in mangion, which for so long have suspected and frowned upon each other. It opens to view Truth as an harmonious unit, and changes general discord into harmony, even though all its vibrations may not yet be understood. In its last analysis, it does away with evil, *per se*, as an entity; for while admitting it as an apparent and relative *condition*, it finds in its unripened and imperfect stage the potency and promise of endless progression and unfoldment. Is this outline visionary? Not in the least, but rather scientific in the highest and best sense of that term. The sidelights and reflections from every possible direction here converge and come to a focus.

All the factors discovered from this corrected point of view not only fit each other, but go far to classify and interpret all the phenomena of the human soul.

THE DIVINITY OF NATURE.

NATURE speaks to us in a language of her own. If her intonations sound harsh or unmusical, we may infer that our hearing is not attuned to her utterances. If her voices are unknown tongues, we need carefully to study her rhythm and accent, in order that we may translate her message. Nature is not Nature until we awaken the spirit of interpretation. We are unable to understand her motive until we take her into our confidence, and make her intimate acquaintance.

What is Nature, and what does she signify to us? What is her kingdom, and where its boundaries? Do we really see her, or only her signs and outpicturings? Is she essentially color, form, proportion, length and breadth, or life, mind, and spirit?

Nature is a revelator. The kingdom of spirit is co-extensive with her dominion, and shines through it. Each is the complement of the other, without boundary line. A poet of keen insight confides to us that —

>'Earth's crammed with heaven,
> And every common bush afire with God;
> But only he who sees takes off his shoes."

Truth must be a full-orbed unit, else she is untruthful. The physicist, while studying forms and properties, may be color-blind to the presence of a universal spiritual dominion. Dissociated from her vital essence, Nature is incongruous and misleading. The materialist interprets her as mechanical, cold, and even cruel. The scientist tests her qualities, and geometrizes her proportions, but does not hear her voices. The theologian, with eyes turned toward the supernatural, does not feel her warm, vital supports and inter-relations to the spiritual realm. Even the artist often catches only her complexion, while her warm and friendly temperament is unrecognized. Each thereby makes his own system misleading and unnatural. Only the spiritual chemism of the poet and idealist divines her affinities, and penetrates to her true inwardness.

The attempt to turn Religion away from Nature, into an arbitrary and unrelated realm, has drained it of its normal and abounding vitality; and, on the other hand, the materialism of Science has kept *its* gaze turned steadily downward. To the practical vision of the world the supernatural is unnatural, and the unnatural, morbid. Nothing unnatural can be attractive. Religion and science have each been weighted down as they have diverged from the normality of the established divine order.

Religion, in its normal simplicity, may be defined as orderly unfoldment which brings into manifestation the divine pattern. The natural world, in its methods and transmutations, is an articulation of the Father. The genius of Nature is an open gospel for all who can decipher its unrolled manuscript. But only the key of the spiritual intuition can unlock the motives and mysteries of cosmic forces, and disclose their beneficent order and rhythm.

The divinity in man recognizes its eternal counterpart, — God in Nature, — and feels the ecstatic thrill of the Omnipresent Spirit. Divine monograms and hieroglyphics are stamped upon all his environment, and he dwells in a boundless repository of mystery, harmony, and sanctity. As our spiritual vision grows clearer, the objective universe takes on intrinsic gracefulness and sublimity. The mirror of an uplifted consciousness reflects new revelations of cosmic harmony and unity. God is the mind of Nature. He whispers to us in every leaf, flower, and blade of grass; in the air, the clouds, the sunshine, the sea. All are eloquent from within. Each is a glowing sentence in the great open volume of universal Scripture. As the sea contains all its waves, so the One Life embraces all finite forms of vitality. This concept is a warm and living spiritual theism, and has no alliance with pantheism. Everything is soulful. Shapes and colors are delightful to the degree that we grasp their plasticity to spiritual moulding from within. Pope's familiar lines are more than poetry: —

> "All are but parts of one stupendous whole,
> Whose body nature is, and God the soul."

As our physical organism is moulded and directed by the mind within, so the whole creation is permeated and vitalized by the immanent God. Emerson, the great modern idealist, thus discourses of expression: —

> "All form is an effect of character; all condition of the quality of life. Here we find ourselves, suddenly, not in a critical speculation, but in a holy place, and should go very warily and reverently. We stand before the secret of the world, there where Being passes into Appearance, and Unity into Variety. The universe is an externalization of the soul. Since everything in nature answers to a moral power, if any phenomenon remains brute and dark, it is because the corresponding faculty in the observer is not yet active."

If we delve deeply enough into the laws and constitution of rocks, plants, animals, and man, we everywhere discover the footprints of the unifying and energizing Presence. The revelations of Deific wisdom and spiritual vitality are as scientifically accurate as they are æsthetically transcendent. To feel our spiritual oneness and relativity to all things, is to expel infelicity and leanness from our consciousness. Such a transformation is, in itself, evidence of the truth of the principle. Nature is friendly. Her correspondences with us are so intimate and reciprocal, that they demonstrate infinite wisdom, unity, and adaptability. Bryant, in his "Thanatopsis," beautifully moulds this thought in his familiar lines: —

THE DIVINITY OF NATURE.

> "To him who in the love of Nature holds
> Communion with her visible forms, she speaks
> A various language; for his gayer hours
> She has a voice of gladness, and a smile
> And eloquence of beauty, and she glides
> Into his darker musings, with a mild
> And healing sympathy, that steals away
> Their sharpness, ere he is aware."

The barrenness and untruthfulness of atheism are evident from their utter inability to awaken human responsiveness. Nothing is abnormal save that which is created by man's defective and misplaced consciousness. He alone can cloud his own horizon. The much-vaunted achievements of material science cannot lift the load of human woe, or satisfy the universal soul-hunger. Whatever is unnatural is a distortion of the divine type. The deadly upas of artificialism is a blight upon literature, society, and institutions. A debasing so-called realism, claiming to be artistic, raises a false and perverted standard in the measurement of fiction, the drama, and real life. To paint abnormity in picturesque and vivid outline is a perversion of true art. Only that which is divine and normal in type can possess veritable artistic proportion. Even intellectual development, as usually defined, is powerless to lift men above the plane of shadows and illusions.

With an arbitrary and materialistic treatment Nature is severed from her vital relations, and becomes a caricature, mechanical, cold, and even adverse. The over-wrought refinements of a hyper-civilization, which subtly beckon us away from the natural type, promise much, but finally end in chaotic degeneration. The blandishments of fashion, society, display and ambition seductively whisper their charms; but following close in their train are barrenness, bitterness and heartlessness. As institutions take on abnormal shape and character, they invite decay. Civilizations, even when most distinguished for material grandeur and æsthetic culture, become top-heavy, and fall, because they lack a simple but broad archetypal basis.

We are touched on every side with life. The outward forms of buds and leaves and flowers may wither and fade from our sight, but the life which for a while held them in form is not lost, but conserved for further expression in yet sweeter and nobler shapes. New worlds are continually created before us for fuller revelations of truth. Every changing season opens fresh vistas, and slips new slides into the lenses of subjectivity which open outwards. Divine laws are engraven all about us, and each is interpreted through its own chosen and particular symbol. Nature has its parables and precepts, its comedies and tragedies. The Decalogue, psalmody, prophecy, the incarnation, sacrifice, and resurrection, are objectively written in living characters all about us, and subjectively inscribed in exact correspondence in the tablets of man's constitution. There are platforms and pulpits on every hand, from each of which is expounded the divine completeness of the established order. Poesy bids us:—

> "Find tongues in trees, books in running brooks,
> Sermons in stones, and good in everything."

That vision is inspired which beholds mountains, forests, and rocks as cathedrals and altars, which enshrine the divine bounty and radiance. We are walking upon enchanted ground, and bushes are aflame all about us, and yet are not consumed.

Arcadian simplicity always has been a saving force, an instinctive feeling after the divine life. The primitive Aryan made Nature his inspiration, and its vigorous power was long perceptible during his migrations and shifting conditions.

A true translation of Nature is not a mental construction, an allegory, or a fancy, but a vision of a living reality working out its grand purpose. We should not read her superficially, as a shallow critic may read a book, with eyes only for its style and construction, but with open soul for her vital meaning and interpretation. But she is shy of her richness, and must be wooed and followed by sympathetic association, in order that she may respond with hearty communication. To pursue her with a mathematical chart, or an intellectual measuring-stick, is to chill and alienate her, so that from a warm and loving mother she becomes only a conventional stranger, made up of mechanical powers and forces.

To the penetrative vision of the Hebrew prophets, Nature was but a transparent medium, through which they clearly saw the Infinite. The fervid imagery of Isaiah gave tongues and voices to every animate thing, and all joined in a universal anthem of praise.

But, as a whole, a sombre shadow overcasts the sacred Hebraistic literature. The Deity was infinite physical force, more than omnipresent Spirit and Love. With an exuberant poetic and artistic symbolism, there is lacking that broader and grander consciousness of divine harmony, unity, and goodness with which a truer concept thrills the soul. Human fellowship and oneness with the spirit of Nature is a later and higher ideal than that of the Old Testament poets and seers.

During the long and gloomy period between the decay of classic culture and the Renaissance, inspiration through Nature almost ceased. The rigid austerity and asceticism which cast their shadows over the Middle Ages obliterated the beauty and harmony of the visible creation. Under such a cloud Nature appeared cold, arbitrary, and forbidding. Men found nothing lovable without, because they were conscious of no beauty within. Men and women barred themselves into cells, and lived behind bare walls, and put God's beautiful world out of sight. The visible universe, stripped of the living Divinity, was stern and joyless. The Deity was loveless, Nature a desert, humanity an object-lesson of deformity, life a bed of spikes, and the future a rayless gloom. But with the modern awakening, the mind of man puts off its fetters, and asserts its freedom; existence becomes joyous, and Nature soulful and companionable. When life loses its plasticity, and becomes artificial and conventional, it hardens into rigid forms, and religion becomes an institution, and worship a prescribed service in temples made with hands. The open volume of the Spirit is pushed to the background by scholastic definitions and ecclesiastical authority and ritual. The outward sense is appealed to by imposing ceremonial, but the divine overflowing in the soul is smothered amid literal structure and objective dogma.

The forces of Nature are the exponents and ministers of righteousness. The man who violates the moral law ignores the principles of his own being, and sets at naught the laws which are inscribed in his inner constitution. It is impossible to cheat or baffle the established order. There is one orderly and beautiful pathway of progress, and no climbing up on the outside. But infinite forces work *with* us when we work *through* them. Nothing is detached, nothing casual, nothing unimportant; but all are necessary to the complete unity. The poet assures us that, —

"The course of Nature is the art of God."

The scale of Nature is boundless. Upward and downward her octaves are endless in vibratory harmony. When we attempt any intellectual solution of her mysteries, we are confronted with the incomprehensibility of the Absolute. But what we cannot rationally measure, we may become one with. The spiritual perception may be filled with its love and goodness, and thoroughly taste its quality.

"Canst thou by searching find out God?" Through the intellect never, but through the inner vision thou mayst see him. God and Nature can only be known through related unisons. Man can cognize them because he has their samples in his soul. He translates them because he has found their subjective key. Said that great interpreter of Nature, Thoreau, in speaking of an experience in the woods: "I was sensible of such a sweet and beneficent society in Nature, in the very pattering in the drops, and in every sight and sound around my house, an infinite and unaccountable friendliness all at once like an atmosphere sustaining me, as made the fancied advantages of human neighborhood insignificant, and I have never thought of them since. Every little pine-needle expanded and swelled with sympathy and befriended me. I was so distinctly made aware of the presence of something kindred to me, even in scenes which we are accustomed to call wild and dreary, and also that the nearest of blood to me, and humanist, was not a person nor a villager, that I thought no place could ever seem strange to me again."

And again: "The indescribable innocence and beneficence of Nature — of sun and wind and rain, of summer and winter — such health, such cheer, they afford forever! and such sympathy have they ever with our race, that all Nature would be affected, and the sun's brightness fade, and the winds would sigh humanely, and the clouds rain tears, and the woods shed their leaves and put on mourning in midsummer, if any man should ever for a just cause grieve. Shall I not have intelligence with the earth?"

One more thought of his: "In a pleasant spring morning all men's sins are forgiven. Such a day is a truce to vice. While such a sun holds out to burn, the vilest sinner may return. Through our own recovered innocence we discern the innocence of our neighbors."

Emerson says that Beauty is a creator; a notable specimen of his divine definitions. Objective loveliness is really soul-reflection. The graceful and perfect forms, colors, odors, and harmonies that we see and feel, are our higher and more ideal thought-pictures, which are painted by the vibrations of Divinity upon our responsive souls. The beauty of a flower consists of the beautiful thought about it. The peculiar quality of things depends not upon intellectual observation, nor even interpretation, but upon the optics of soul.

A potato-patch in full blossom to one means only coming potatoes, to another an æsthetic revelation of Divinity.

How exquisitely does Nature do her finishing, polishing, and shading! No point-laces, brocades, or velvets can compare with her embroidery in lichens, ferns, and mosses. Her shuttles weave more delicate fabrics than those fashioned by the cunning of the looms and dyes of the Orient.

Man mars and cuts her fair face; but she uncomplainingly hastens to hide, soften, and repair his rude angles and scars. Even our beautiful country roads, which she trims with soft and variegated fringes, delighting the eye and soul of the wayfarer, are mowed and squared by crude human artificiality. But she, the beautifier and healer, follows with her magic touch of restoration. Everything is beautiful. The science of the world could not fashion the petal of a flower, the sting of a bee, nor the point of a thistle. The polish of a grain of sand is infinite. Every natural thing is a revelation of the skill and taste of the Divine Artist.

Various kinds of matter are really different modes of motion, each having its peculiar vibration. The most real and solid thing in the universe — if there be anything other than universal spirit — is the illimitable ether, which to sense is unknown except through some of its effects. Paradoxical as it may seem, while it is the most solid of all things, it is also the most elastic. John Fisk, in his "Unseen World," says of it: "It fills all material bodies like a sea, in which the atoms are as islands, and it occu-

THE DIVINITY OF NATURE.

pies the whole of what we call empty space. It is so sensitive, that a disturbance in any part of it causes a tremor which is felt on the surface of countless worlds." But the qualities which we attribute to objective conditions are really in us, and do not touch the absolute, or, we may better say, spiritual realities.

Material science in the past has insisted that mind and spirit can only be known in their activities and phenomena through or in connection with a material base or organization. Such a conclusion is now outlawed, and the latest and highest trend of physics is now all in the other direction. Spirit is the reality, and matter its servant and sensuous expression. The seen universe or world of sense is only a parable, or a realm of show, like shadow-pantomime, indicative of the character of realities behind. Spenser aptly puts this thought: —

> "So every spirit, as it is more pure,
> And hath in it the more of heavenly light,
> So it the fairer body doth procour
> To habit in, and it more fairly dight,
> With cheerful grace and amiable sight.
> For of the soul, the body form doth take,
> For soul is form, and doth the body make."

To the degree in which we are spiritually unfolded, we may penetrate beyond appearance, and gain glimpses of the real. Our eyes have never looked upon our friend, nor even upon our very selves, but only upon manifestations and coverings.

We see but little of the spiritual world in Nature, because our finer faculties are only in an infantile stage of development. But even among physical existences our sensuous and intellectual range is so limited, that modern science admits that there may be whole universes of beings who dwell among us, or pass through us, of whose presence we know nothing. Their forms, colors, and properties are so subtle, that only beings whose senses are far more acute than ours can be introduced into their society. What ranges of orders upon orders above and below us! An eminent scientist has recently made the startling suggestion, that not only below us may exist molecular universes, intelligences, and even civilizations, but that above us perhaps worlds may be but as molecules of grand systems and organizations.

But such speculations in physical science have no especial value, unless by way of analogy they quicken our perception of the spiritual verities, of which the visible universe is but the printed page. O man, made in God's image, and linked to and nourished by Nature, what glorious vistas are to open before you in the eons of eternal progress!

Nature is God and love and truth translated. The world is embellished by spirit, and its inaudible music is the cadence of the gospel of good-will. Nature is a vast kindergarten, where easy object-lessons train our child-like affections so they may gain strength to finally mount above and beyond them. As to her teaching, says Wordsworth: —

> "One impulse from a vernal wood
> May teach you more of man,
> Of moral evil and of good,
> Than all the sages can."

The latest movements of science in prying into Nature's deeper subtleties are a reproof to former conventionalism and finished materialistic concepts. A truer realism is coming to claim the spiritual genesis of all normal types; their spontaneity, perfection, and vital warmth. Art is becoming purified of arbitrary conventions, and with a free and plastic movement falling into the rhythm of divine harmonies and patterns. When so inspired she is the handmaid of spiritual development. Whether in the groined arches and Gothic tree-like forms which are materialized in grand cathedrals, or in the ideal of the sculptor, which, like Galatea, is ready to burst into life, or on glowing canvas instinct with stories of living reality, art is the visible moulder of idealism and the revealer of faith.

The human imagination, freed from the leaden weights of pessimism, pathology, and literal limitation, soars aloft into the upper atmosphere of light and growth. The revelation of divinity in Nature is in exact accord with that which is incarnated in the Son. God is the author of all truth, and therefore every realm is sacred. The unperverted type of normal man, as seen in the Christ, confirms the inherent oneness of God and his children. The beautiful proportions of the perfect human model demonstrate that a full influx of the divine life tempers all the fancies of the imagination and impulses of the will to a heavenly shaping; and this is full-grown man — the measure of the stature of the Christ. The revelation of God in Nature is not less sacred than that through the Son or the Book. It is a great volume of pictorial illustration, at the centre of which man himself is the grandest feature.

"The groves were God's first temples."

The simplicity, freedom, and spontaneity of the early religions were manifested in a sympathetic oneness with Nature, and an instinctive feeling of her divinity. The people assembled for worship or sacrifice at natural shrines, or under the broad canopy of heaven, rather than in temples made with hands.

In process of time, as sacred enclosures, synagogues, and temples became common, men began to feel that in a special way these structures contained God, and that there was little divinity outside. Instead of being omnipresent, as men proclaimed with their lips, in their feelings He was either divided and limited, or else far away. They could only awaken their sense of Him at special times and in particular places. The consciousness was still further limited to set ordinances, sacraments,

THE DIVINITY OF NATURE.

and ceremonies. God consecrated all things, and yet men so lost an appreciation of the overwhelming presence, that only those particular places and environments are regarded sacred which men, through their own special, puny forms, reconsecrate.

But we would have no place less sacred, but lift all up to the high level and ideal. Men have effectively deconsecrated nature, art, institutions, customs, and even our own physical organisms, which have been truly declared to be temples of the Holy Ghost.

We have drawn a sharp line around a few things which we have identified with God, pronouncing everything outside of these secular. We have virtually shut him out of all religions except our own, and, through a limited inspiration, out of all books save one. We have dispensed with him in history, with the exception of the doings of one race; and so, not feeling his particular presence in other records, have rated them as profane. We have, perhaps unwittingly, almost declared that God could not be found outside of one institution, one system, one round of observances and saving ordinances. We have not so intended, but our anthropomorphic and limited ideas of our Deity have logically closed the portal of the higher consciousness.

The church and the Bible are good, but are not all. We may truly meet God in the groves or fields, on the mountain-top, under the azure canopy, or by the shimmering sea; but, as we are constituted in his image, most nearly, face to face, in the sanctuary of our own soul.

We go to meet him one day in seven, but he is with us all days, and upon invitation will dwell in our living consciousness. True thinking, service, and aspiration are profitable on Monday as well as on Sunday.

We have put God out of business, out of politics, out of political economy, out of education, and out of society, and thereby made them Godless. Encased in our sensuous pursuits, we fail to feel him, though he besets us behind and before, and is nearer than our thoughts. Only his immanence explains all the marvels of nature within and around us. Not merely worship, but communion and fellowship with the "All in All," should be the noblest, sweetest, truest, purest experience of life.

We can lift everything towards the divine by transforming our own ideals. "The pure in heart shall see God." What a wonderful power and privilege! and yet it potentially belongs to all. How often we have rated this grand declaration as metaphor or allegory, rather than as scientific exact truth.

Life, in all forms and on all planes, is a direct deific manifestation. There is only one vitality, but it is all-inclusive.

The materialist sees nature only as a great mechanism. His standpoint will not permit of the broader

THE DIVINITY OF NATURE.

range of reality. He views the prismatic glory of the rainbow merely as light resolved, the beauty of leaf and flower only as chemical selection, and bursting and exuberant life only as a response to light, heat, and moisture. Nature to him is therefore a hopeless, loveless, cold, remorseless machine, a general arena of warring forces. But true science, at this late period, is beginning to divine her friendliness. We are learning to listen while she whispers to us of her subtle laws and methods. She is waiting to serve us in every direction. Her very regularity, which we thought was machine-like, we learn to depend upon, and find it beneficent. In our undeveloped state we thought her our enemy. But vibration, with her divine rhythm, causes all things to become ours. She places reins of relationship in our hands, which reach out objectively in all directions.

We often speak of the forces of Nature. But back of all forces there is one Force; back of all laws, one Law; back of all causes, one Cause, one Spirit, one Life, one Love.

THE HYGIENE OF THE CONSCIOUSNESS.

The scope of material hygiene, though important in itself, is essentially partial and incomplete. There is another great causative domain which is both higher and complementary, and it is unwise to ignore it.

As compared with any former period, modern investigation is inclined to delve deeply in order to discover hidden principles, and to reach inward to primary causation; or, in other words, to get at the soul of things. The science of sanitation naturally feels the general stimulus above noted. It is becoming increasingly evident that a mere external observance of hygienic regulation does not necessarily make everything clean within. Great progress has been made from a blind reliance upon drugs as an antidote for human ills, toward a prevention of them through physical hygiene; and this important step is creditable and profitable. But progress never ceases, and a further extension of hygienic effort is clearly in order. Attention is being more and more directed from the objective towards the subjective, from the seen towards the unseen, and from things towards thoughts.

The effects of the application of material remedies for physical ills, as variously utilized, have been exhaustively studied, and endless experiments made, without marked or radical success. Theories and methods in *materia medica* are still largely experimental and tentative.

It has been practically assumed that the human constitution is to be dealt with as a fixed quantity and quality; and investigation has almost entirely spent itself upon supposed remedies from without, rather than upon prevention, and in combating symptoms rather than in finding causes. The question has been, as to just the effect of this or that drug, and more recently this or that temperature, humidity, exercise, climate, and physical habit, upon the assumed human fixture. That the conditions just named are important may be admitted; but the question is, Can that supposed fixture or human ego be so modified *in itself*, that it will come into different relations with its environment? Every accomplishment is a growth, and it is found that the individual can become increasingly independent of external conditions, so as not to always be "under the circumstances." Man is not a material mechanism, but a living entity working from within.

The principle that deserves recognition is, that the order of causation is from the mental and spiritual internal, toward the correspondential and expressive physical external.

It has been abundantly proved that anger changes the secretions; that fear deranges the circulation and deteriorates the blood; that anxiety wastes the nervous energy; and that selfishness, pessimism, and immoral thought drain and impoverish the vitality. These things and many others make it evident that nothing in man is *fixed*, but rather that the subjective realm is the promising field for new observation and effort.

Outward occasions of human ills have been mistakenly regarded as their primary causes. A more correct estimate is that physical characteristics are only the visible index or exponent of the living, moulding internal forces. And further, it is increasingly evident that cultivated thought, emotion, and consciousness modify physical expression and condition. Mere occasions may *offer* us ills, but it is susceptibility that takes them in and succumbs to them.

Hygiene, to be truly scientific, must begin to concern itself with the cleanness of mind as well as body, and with the ventilation of the thought-atmosphere as well as with that of the apartment. Bad mental pictures must be classed with sewer-gas, and pessimism rated as malaria. Idealism and spiritual optimism must take their place among sanitarian agencies, and man utilize his hitherto slumbering resources and focalize his thought-forces. The vitality can be invigorated and stimulated from *within*.

A thorough mental hygiene means more than an outward formal conformity to respectable ethical standards. The thought-habits and resting-places must be intelligently chosen. Ideals that we are to gain an intimacy with must be selected with the same, and even greater care than we exercise in the choice of personal associates. What one thinks most about, he either becomes or grows like, and it is the tendency and function of the physical organism to mirror it forth. Let us, then, train our minds to focalize themselves upon those qualities and things that we wish to manifest, rather than upon what we would like to avoid.

We should build a thought-realm of ideals of harmony, health, soundness, and sanity *now*, and not put them off to a hoped-for future. If at present the body is not expressing such conditions, the inner perfect reality must be firmly held until, at length, it is projected into outward expression. We are souls having bodies, and not bodies having souls. Man is above his visible instrument, or embodiment, and should continually affirm his rule of it. The reverse is slavery. "As a man thinketh in his heart so is he." By an understanding of the law of mental concentration he may gradually change his consciousness concerning himself. Thereby he increasingly dominates physical sensation, and by degrees frees himself from its tyranny. Mental hygiene, therefore, includes the intelligent cultivation of a new and higher self-consciousness. Such a compliance with higher law is thoroughly normal, wholesome, and in accord with man's constitution. As he lifts himself into the calm occupation of the higher selfhood, things that have been adverse and rebellious fall into friendly and harmonious service. He thereby grasps the reins of objective relationship, and comes into possession of his legal and rightful heritage.

WHAT IS MAN?

WE are living in a remarkable era. In these closing years of the nineteenth century the minds of men are restless as never before. Systems, philosophies, theories, and institutions are being questioned, shaken, and summoned to the judgment-bar of truth. A gigantic pair of balances, real though immaterial, has been set up; and not only persons, but principles, customs, methods, and dogmas, are being newly weighed, re-appraised, and re-valued. Men are diligently searching for the *summum bonum* with an unwonted vigor.

Not longer content to supinely yield to adversities and ills, as belonging to the lot of humanity, — inevitable, and to be tamely submitted to, — there is a rapidly growing disposition to question, yes even to deny, their supremacy, and to sweep away the great mass of self-imposed limitations of the past, that have no valid reason for existence.

The search for truth, and the higher appreciation of its supernal value, were never before so intense and universal. As a dominant force, principles and spiritual ideals are taking the place of external authorities, dogmas, and theories. The divinely established order, when correctly interpreted, is found to be, not cold, or merely neutral, but positively beneficent. Mankind, therefore, is discovering that conformity to law not only eliminates and dissipates human ills, but more; that it brings positive reward and harmony.

The nature of man, in its essence, is not only one of the most interesting of topics, but, more than that, is supremely practical and vital. The problems which are centred in, and arise from that complex nature, are so near, so all-inclusive and supreme, that they incomparably overshadow all others. Unlike the vast majority of conventional systems and philosophies, they are not merely speculative and objective, but have to do with the very heart and soul of divinity and humanity. Upon a correct or incorrect interpretation of these laws of relationship, their subtle action, interaction and reaction, depend human progress and happiness, or stagnation and decadence.

What, then, is man? If we listen for a practical response to this question from the consensus of world opinions, thoughts, pursuits, and activities, we learn that man is an animated fleshly statue, visible, sensuous, and material. Nine-tenths of all the labor, ingenuity, and effort of human kind are put forth in ministration to this visible man. He is ruler of this realm, and receives universal homage. His wants are supplied, his appetites pampered, his inclinations deferred to, his vanity stimulated, and his whims yielded to, until he becomes a life-sized exaggeration and abnormity. It is thought that so long as he has desirable food, clothing, shelter, material comfort and luxury, supplemented with some intellectual development, he should be complete and content. If he lack any of these things, he must be kindly supplied with them, and then he ought to be satisfied. But he is not. This so-called man is never happy, but always just about to be. He follows his own fancied ideal untiringly; but it is ever a little in advance, just beyond his grasp. Science is always about to add something more to his physical accomplishments, and then all will be well. When he travelled in the stage-coach, if he could have had just a glimpse of the future limited express, he would have exclaimed, "I then shall be happy!" Electrical invention, with all its multiform miracles of improvement, promised much; but in spite of all these and other grand inventions men have steadily grown more uneasy. This self-styled man is now looking forward to aerial navigation, higher technical education, improved legislation, sanitation, and medication, as the things yet needed for human perfection. These realized, all will be serene. He bows the knee to all the sensuous forces of science, and believes, in the words of one of its great exponents, that "all potency is contained in matter."

But in other moods this apparent man expects to find all completeness which is yet lacking in new institutions or improved external forms of government. Some patent social system, land system, tax system, or monetary system is to heal prevailing ills, abolish poverty, prevent crime and ignorance, and usher in general felicity and harmony.

Every road is traversed, and every by-way explored, in order to again find and restore the complete satisfaction of a sensuous Eden. But fixed in the established evolutionary order, there is a "flaming sword" which turns every way, and this forever bars the road back to a material paradise; nay, even more, it renders impossible the attainment of any supreme felicity of a mere social or intellectual order. The insurmountable obstacle is subjective,— entirely within,— and consists in the truth that this man that we have described is not really man at all. It is only his shadow, his material expression, his visible instrument.

He has mistaken his own identity. His woes, failures, restlessness, and unhappiness all come from the fact that he believes himself to be material in his being. He has formed the habit of feeling that his body is himself. Through this state of consciousness he has come into servitude to sin, disease, and death, and innumerable other limitations and infelicities. In a word, he is filled with a subtle soul-hunger which he is unable to diagnose or interpret. While all good in their order, neither morality, social reform, temperance, ethical culture, nor intellectualism, one or all, reaches deeply enough to cure the inner craving. That which has been earnestly pursued as a veritable *summum bonum* turns out to be an *ignis fatuus*, which ever lures men more deeply into a materialistic wilderness.

It is true that when stated as an abstract doctrine many would hold that they are not body; but so long as they practically act and feel that way, the material consciousness is ruling, and its corresponding inharmonious fruitage appears. The disastrous effects of such a radical misapprehension are not diminished by conventional education nor so-called intellectual development. The mistaken self-conscious imagery of a highly cultivated quality is as thoroughly imbued with restlessness — often more so — than that of much lower attainment.

Logic and philosophy, though located in a higher department, are still within the limits of that inferior evolutionary kingdom where conscious or unconscious misplacement is ever present. Even eminent morality and altruism may exist without spiritual activity and illumination.

The man that has been outlined, consisting of a visible upright form, is not a counterfeit, but a correspondential index or counterpart. He bears the same relation to the real that a figure does to the number. The external sign is useful in its place, but it *is* something only as it represents something. The physical man only plays a character in shadow pantomime. A personality is beheld, but the real ego or individuality is unmanifest until the spiritual consciousness is unfolded.

No man has ever seen his friend, or even himself. It is the unseen which is the real and substantial. The world has been mistaken in regarding man as a material being. This belief is the basic reason for his ever-present frictions and trials. He expects to be a soul after a certain event called death, but that he is the same here and now does not occur to him. "One world at a time," he says, which on the surface seems quite logical. But in reality one world is all there is. The thought environment — which is the nearest and only reality — remains unchanged, regardless of the mutations which may overtake visible expression.

Is then the body bad, and are we advocating a morbid asceticism? Just the reverse. The material organism is good, and altogether real as expression, in its normal relation and position. The mistake is in identity, which is a radical misplacement. At first sight this error would not appear serious, but a deeper view reveals momentous distinctions and consequences. Let us note some of the effects of this false consciousness.

In the first place, it creates its own morbid conditions. Whether the man or the body be enthroned makes a world-wide difference. One must rule, and the other serve. If this question be settled in accord with the divinely established order, both are good and harmonious. Then they just fit and supplement each other. But if the ego be identified in the consciousness with the sensuous, or even with the intellectual nature, it takes on innumerable limitations, and yields a slavish subjugation.

We are not now making exclusive reference to those whose physical propensities are rampant, like profligates, drunkards, and sensualists, but to the average individual whose outward life is in accord with prevailing ethical standards. It is obvious that the deeper the depravity the more absolute the bondage; but the vital question presents itself, Is any real bondage normal or necessary? True, complete and immediate emancipation from the mistakes and false consciousness of the past — stamped upon us as it is by habit, heredity, and universal suggestive environment — is unattainable. Such is not the method of evolutionary growth.

But granting that it must be gradual to our apprehension, how can it be hastened and made sure? If the remedy for the woes and disorders of the world be contained in a new or reformed consciousness which is based upon a recognition of the real selfhood, or intrinsic divinity of constitution, how can this radical departure be brought about? The answer is evident. Man must begin to think rightly of himself. He must build up an entire new thought world through self-formed ideals held in his own willing subject the body exercises a sweet ministry and useful service for its owner, and becomes an outward reflector and translator of mental and spiritual harmony.

The vital and unseen forces build the body, and not the body the forces. The thought forms the brain, and not the brain the thought. The visible form is the stereotype plate, cast from the fused immaterial composition of past mental states. Matter, whether erected into vegetal, animal, or human configurations, is moulded and qualified by the soul-forging which goes on within.

Let us inquire for a moment as to the necessity for some more potent energy than that afforded by conventional means for the healing of prevalent maladies and the overcoming of human ills and weaknesses. Do we find that these are fleeing away? and are we satisfied to rest in past attainments? Is it not desirable to occupy a more elevated vantage-ground, from which we may effectively charge and drive out the multiform host of abnormal and perverse intruders?

Even hygiene has but a limited range, so long as man fails to study the laws of his own being, and gives all his attention to external conditions. He critically examines and analyzes every known thing, "in the heavens above, the earth beneath, and the waters under the earth," except the one thing most important, — his own constitution. The more deeply he penetrates into the apparent complexity of adverse environment, the more discouraging and hopeless the outlook. Every new discovery lures him more deeply into a materialistic bog. So soon as one hostile element is vanquished, another yet more subtle is found concealed in ambush behind it. From the sensuous standpoint, humanity is menaced within and without.

The germ-theory has brought a mental picture of innumerable hostile organisms which are supposed to be lying in wait for our destruction. But in reality the great majority of these are friendly; and those that seem otherwise, when not scavengers, are concomitants or effects rather than causes. Pathology becomes so abnormal that the very elements are rated as antagonistic. Hygiene is invoked to ward off all these numerous ills which fear, expectation, and acceptance have armed.

But in the present state of human consciousness, collectively, we have to yield to some limitations which past and present belief has imposed. In the cases of contagions and epidemics, quarantines and barriers must be imposed until there is a general affirmation of freedom. We are, in measure, bound by laws of our own imposing until there is a general emancipation. *Collective* improvement can therefore only be gradual and evolutionary.

But the ideal to develop is that of an inner and spiritual armor — as scientific as it is spiritual —

field of vision. This virtually means a new personality and a new environment. The material for this new creation is contained in an intelligent projected volume of thought in accord with the higher law.

To overcome the crass materialism in which the world is at present inthralled, man must continually affirm, not only to his fellows, but to himself, that he is a spiritual, and not a material, entity. He must iterate and reiterate this great truth, until it is supremely installed in the kingdom of mind. He is not a body having a soul, but a soul having a body. The formative power of thought makes this change of consciousness revolutionary.

As man truly recognizes himself, assumes the prerogatives of his divine being, and knows that he is a spiritual dynamo here and now, he wields new forces, and grasps supernal powers and privileges. He comes into at-one-ment with the primal and deific creative principle, and, from a condition of vassalage, finds himself a prince of the realm.

By virtue of his subjective transformation he has established new relations with the objective world; and now laws and conditions pay him tribute instead of exacting it. He has become a spiritual alchemist, and through the alembic of the divinity awakened within him is able to transmute the seeming "common and unclean" into the pure, the ideal, and the God-like. He is able to know and demonstrate the beneficence of the established order, and to adjust himself to it.

He has divined that there is no such objective principle as evil, and that that which has been so denominated is only a subjective distortion, which can be displaced, and thereby rendered non-existent. Enlisting all law in his behalf, through an understanding of, and compliance with its methods, he uses it as though it were his own. He re-enforces himself with supernal and cosmic energy by thinking God's thoughts after him.

But let us more specifically attempt to translate this new consciousness, or higher thought, into near and concrete application and expression. This new philosophy of life and being is no fine-spun metaphysical abstraction, but of the utmost practicality and utility in every-day living. We may first inquire, What does it do for the body, that most useful instrument which man has so persistently mistaken for himself?

The illuminated intuitive perception soon confers such a sense of spiritual supremacy and harmony that, as a natural result, the body increasingly expresses hearty co-operation and wholeness. It is the one thing necessary for its own welfare that it should glide into its secondary, befitting, and normal position. Its dethronement from the *rôle* of a tyrannical ruler is the very act which works out its own salvation.

"Order is heaven's first law;" therefore misplacement is lawless, disorderly, and destructive. As a

OUR RELATIONS TO ENVIRONMENT.

The threads which connect us with objective things are woven into our life-fabric, and determine its quality. This is true in its application alike to circumstances, events, principles, and persons. We are not only influenced and modified by relations, but are made by them. The ego is the vital centre of a network of derived, shared, and related ties over which vibrations are continually passing. The ideal condition to be sought is harmony with the cosmic order.

It is apparent that if the quality of relations determines character, a consideration of our power to modify and improve them becomes of great importance. There are but two possible ways in which changes in our relations to the external world can take place. One involves an alteration in the objective things or circumstances themselves, — either through our own efforts or those of others, — and the other, a change in ourselves, or in our attitude and disposition towards them.

We find, however, that our power to reconstruct, or even to modify, outside conditions, in order to mould them to our liking, is exceedingly limited.

To improve our external surroundings we may, perhaps, move from place to place, and thus find new conditions and society; but even when this is practicable, it does not always furnish the desired improvement. Our duties or business will not always admit of such experiments, even if they were uniformly successful. In removing ourselves from the presence of seeming ills, we are liable "to fly to others which we know not of."

But our closest and most real environment is that of our own mentality, or thought world, which we carry with us, and which cannot be readily altered by a mere change of locality. A moment's consideration will show that a vast majority of the ills that encompass us are of our own making, and belong to our own economy. They are not a real part of us, however, though they may often seem so to be.

Our limited ability to control external conditions so as to ideally shape and color them, makes it evident that the main field for improvement lies at our own end of the lines of relationship. From our spiritual centre or ego radiate lines which connect us with every part of the universe of God. Invisible telegraphic wires keep us in communication with every material object and spiritual entity, and currents of attraction or repulsion are ever crossing over them. Everything is sending its message to us. The stars, the sky, the cloud, the air, heat, cold, the landscape, the flower, — each and all are transmitting their communications to our consciousness. Events, transactions, joys, fears, good and ill, all flash their varied and peculiar despatches to the heart of our being, — the ego.

Are we weak and passive recipients of all these discordant sounds? and are we bound to receive them as unwelcome? or can we, in great measure, transform and harmonize their significance? These are not mere questions of curious speculation or metaphysical abstraction, but of intense and living practicality. If it be in any degree possible, through spiritual culture and unfoldment, to improve and rule our relations, rather than to remain in utter subjection to them, we should be alive to such an opportunity and privilege. We frequently say what we will do *"under* the circumstances;" but is there a possibility that we can get *over* the circumstances? Is there a kind of spiritual alchemy at our command, by which the freight of base metal which comes to us over the lines of relationship may be transmuted into the fine gold of utility and harmony?

Spiritual problems, like those of mathematics, are solved by scientific rules because they have a similar exactitude. Let us suggest a proposition which every one may utilize in some degree, and which, if observed, may prove an "open sesame" to higher conditions, and then test it as we try a key in the wards of a lock. *The messages that we receive over all the multiform invisible wires of relationship are the exact reflection and correspondence of those we send out.* Even though we fail to recognize their features, they are of our own design and engraving. Our own thought regarding person, place, state, or thing is flashed back, even though we may not identify it.

Let us try to bring out this principle of universal application by means of a simple illustration. A nervously sensitive person lives upon a noisy city thoroughfare. For some reason it is not practicable for him to remove to a more quiet locality. The roar of traffic over pavements and the buzz of electric cars become intolerable, and prevent repose by day and by night. The sensitive one is antagonized, and sends out a current of unreconciled and rebellious thought, and in return each rumble and buzz telegraphs back its harsh and troublesome message. Now apply the rule. Though at first it seem mechanical, and even absurd, let the sensitive one affirm and send out thoughts: "That noise is music to my ears; that roar is necessary, and it is therefore *good*. It conduces to the convenience of many whose comfort I highly value. It shall *not* be evil to me, for I will make it good. I am learning to love its music, and I will send out no other thought. I actually enjoy it."

Let the nervous person faithfully *persevere* in the course indicated for a few weeks, and see if the roar does not become a veritable lullaby. What a boon if we can transform stumbling-blocks into stepping-stones! We become despondent, and perhaps ill, because we think things are *against* us; and each thing sends back a transcript with the same coloring. Two persons experience similar pains or illnesses. One regards his experience as an unmitigated calamity, undeserved, without good cause, and only evil. Things are *against* him; and he is impatient and rebellious, or else wilts before them. In either case intensity is added. Every sensation thus voices back his own thought. The other person soliloquizes: "This experience is educational and necessary, else it would not exist. All law is beneficent, even that which produced this result; and it must tend toward my spiritual development, and is therefore *good*. I cheerfully accept this teaching, and will profit by it. In the future I will try to avoid past mistakes, and 'think no evil.'" The judgment is thereby *accepted*, the suffering fades out, and the seeming evil becomes a good; and all for the reason that the good thought came back like an harmonious echo.

The law of non-resistance is immutable and divine. "But I say unto you that ye resist not evil: but whosoever shall smite thee on thy right cheek, turn to him the other also." "Absurd!" says the worldly policy. But non-resistance conquers. Rising superior to the affront, it transforms the whole transaction. Again, "Love your enemies," and so they are *overcome* and changed into friends. The "enemy" may not always be a person, but possibly an event, an illness, a seeming calamity, a fear, or misfortune. As soon as messages of love are sent to them, — which may be in the shape of a realization that seeming evils are really good in disguise, — they lose the hostile attitude which they have occupied in our consciousness. They remove their repugnant masks, and are found to be friends. We must resolve that nothing shall antagonize us. Whether here or hereafter, unlimited antagonism is hell. As we repel *things*, they repel us.

But should we not antagonize evil? Only by showing a better way. It may be admitted that in the present evolutionary stage of society, civil governments must possess executive force; but even now the law of non-resistance is available for the individual. As rapidly as unselfishness comes into recognition, not only as the highest, but as the most profitable law, governments will become organized channels for altruism.

In proportion to its intensity, antagonism is suicidal. How many allow trivial matters, even possibly mere questions of taste and fancy, to make them critical and uncomfortable. Individuals, sects, and parties antagonize each other, not so much for what they really are, as for what subjective coloring makes them appear to be. The quality of environment is largely what we make it. If we recognize and emphasize the negative and evil, even with purpose of correction, we not only unwittingly aid in bringing it into manifestation, but we receive it back with interest.

Thought is a projectile which always hits the target; and if silently telegraphed specifically, or even at random, it is gathered up and echoed back in like grade and measure. Love "thinketh no evil" is one of Paul's scientific declarations. We must learn to control our thoughts rather than let them control us. If left to their own free course, without discipline and supervision, then, like a rudderless boat, we become the sport of every passing breeze and current. The will must exercise itself in the selection of right thought material. "With what measure ye mete it shall be measured to you again." This is even a truer philosophy of thought interchange than of transactions of a material nature. Every sound, whether of harmony or discord, has its corresponding echo.

God, being the sum-total of all our other relations, must have our supremest homage and love. Messages of aspiration, oneness, and communion, flashed out from our end of the line of his relationship, come back in vibrations, sweet, heavenly, and harmonious. The law of attraction and correspondence is universal. As sons of God we should, through law, reign over the realms below us. The divine element in humanity is *creative*, and must be exercised. Thus we may evolve good, and bring it into manifestation. While we may not at once be able to attain to that altitude where the universal beneficence of the divine order is fully apparent, we may climb and aspire, and each step will open up a broader horizon of the real.

DIVINITY AND HUMANITY.

> "More near than aught thou call'st thy own,
> Draw if thou canst the mystic line,
> Severing rightly His from thine,
> Which is human, which divine."

WHAT is the normal relation between God and Man? Can there be any distinct boundary line between them? Is there a divine side to man which opens out into the unfathomable deeps of the deific nature? These are the most important questions which can occupy the human consciousness.

History is largely composed of the records of the attempts of humanity to build walls of separation. Men have been continually putting up bars around themselves, leaving God outside. To a great degree they have also shut out Nature and their fellow-men. They have drawn sharp lines between their own souls and the Universal Soul. They have been like pieces of chain disconnected by severed links from anything substantial, or like sections of water-pipe parted from the reservoir. Man's nature, when walled in, becomes a dry and barren desert. There is no freshness, no verdure, no growth. The building of division walls has been so general and so long continued that disunion has become the rule. Not only is divinity excluded, but humanity itself is shattered into fragments.

In the more infantile condition of the race, there seems to have been a divine nearness and intimacy which has been lost. As wealth, power, material improvement, and civilization increased, they usurped the whole mental horizon of mankind. Man has never been destitute of so-called religions, but they gradually became formal and devitalized. To the patriarchs of simple and devout life, God — the Great Unseen — was a present and all-important factor. While their concept of the divine character was limited and low, it was near and real. In ages of Arcadian simplicity, and among the primitive Aryans, Nature was the great revelator, and an intimate sympathy with her harmonies and mysteries freshened and vitalized humanity. Even the pantheism and paganism of the Greeks contained so much of the intuitive element, that Paul declared that God was not far from every one of them. "As certain even of your own poets have said, For we are also his offspring." We owe them perhaps more than we are aware for many high ideals of beauty, purity, and spirituality. God revealed himself through his Son to the Hebrew, and so to the world; but he had always been revealing himself through Nature and the intuition, and this revelation was distinct in the Greek consciousness.

But later, a material artificial civilization sprang up, and formal systems and institutions began to multiply, and increasingly they grew out of touch with the divine and unseen. The intellectual faculty became more highly developed, and it overshadowed the inner perception. The primitive church, pure and spiritual at first, gradually became theological, institutional, and polemic. Scholasticism, always intellectually capricious, formulated system upon system; and each raised a wall of exclusiveness, and shut itself out, not only from divine involution, but from human sympathy and oneness. Divisions and subdivisions, sects and schools, multiplied, each contracting its own domain, and each seeing only a fragment of the universal unity of truth in its field of vision.

Now, for the first time in ages, the process seems to be reversed. Ancient walls are slowly crumbling, and the sweet sunshine of larger truth is dispelling darkness and narrowness, and a unifying charity is dissolving all barriers. The beautiful outlines of God the Father, and Man the Brother, are seen to be not only bright, but near — nay, within. Men are "feeling after God," and finding him. Religion — the binding of man to God — is assuming its vital and original significance; and the binding is waxing stronger on man's part by his growing consciousness of the transcendent beauty and attractiveness of the divine nature, not only in general, but within himself.

The apparent retrograde since the days of Greek

idealism and of primitive Christianity, when the human spiritual perception was relatively in a state of high development, is only a swing of the pendulum, the grander and wider progress being always upward. Spiritual evolution comes unevenly, and through apparent wide vibrations. A seeming suspended development, or even a temporary retrograde, stores up energy to give a new and unprecedented impulse to the pendulum of progress. Times of apparent rest or declension furnish the soil in which new and more luxuriant crops of human attainment mature in the divine sunlight.

The Dispensation of the Spirit comes on apace. That increasing God-consciousness which forms the basis of, and has outward attestation in mental and physical healing, is also manifesting itself in the broadening of theological systems, and in the spiritualizing of science itself. The church is awakening to the fact that she has been deficient in that living experience of spiritual vitality which alone can lift her out of a barren intellectual formalism. Literature is being enriched by a warm influx of lofty idealism which brings out in high relief the deific features of man's inner nature. Science is emerging from its cold, earthy materialism, where it has hibernated, into a marked appreciation, not only of immaterial orderly force, but of unity, design, beneficence, and divine substance. It is now as "scientific" to study the nature and destiny of the human soul as to spend a lifetime in the investigation of bugs, fishes, animals, geology, or astronomy. Man is finding that to *know himself* is at least as valuable an accomplishment as a knowledge of molecules and bacteria. Poetry, which always has had much of the divine sparkle in its melodies, glows with an increasing inspiration. Even fiction is being lifted out of the base realism which, by a false standard, has been rated as "artistic," and is moving like a smooth-running vehicle to convey higher ideals into the living domain of human consciousness.

The disjointed fragments of truth are being gathered up and fitted, each in its place, "without the sound of hammer," into the universal temple. The harmony, inter-relation, and goodness of ALL THINGS are disclosed, and, by a living attraction, they are cemented and unified. The world, by a super-sensuous preception, is feeling God within and around it; and while the Bible is no longer regarded as the *only* channel for revelation, its testimony is confirmed and its spiritual foundations broadened.

The brightened glow of Immanuel carries with it everything that man has lacked for the rounding out of his complex nature. As he discovers the universal beneficent trend pervading both the macrocosm and the microcosm, he finds the manifested God.

HAS MENTAL HEALING A VALID SCIENTIFIC AND RELIGIOUS BASIS?[1]

As this topic is somewhat unconventional, the author may be pardoned for a few preliminaries that are somewhat personal and explanatory. He has no professional interest along this line, his position being that of an independent investigator and seeker for truth. He does not appear as the advocate of any school, system, or cult, but only as one who, from force of circumstances, has been led to some appreciation of great principles, a knowledge of which the world greatly needs.

A personal experience, some years since, of unusual depth and intensity, involving an application of the new philosophy, was the starting-point of a most thorough, impartial, and conservative investigation which has followed. An intense philosophical desire to probe as deeply as possible, without fear or favor, was awakened. With such a vivid subjective attestation of the power of a law not yet generally recognized, no one possessing any altruistic spirit could

[1] Substance of a paper read by invitation before the clergymen's "Monday Club" (Unitarian Ministers of Boston and vicinity) at the Channing Building, Boston, June 3, 1895.

quietly settle down to silence, simply because his own immediate personal needs had been satisfied.

The writer has cultivated conservatism, and even incredulity, in forming conclusions regarding the new thought, which are made up from a careful study of its best literature, philosophy, and practical demonstrations. The fact that he has felt impelled to write somewhat upon this much misunderstood subject, as one of its results, has brought an extensive correspondence, in which are included accounts of a great number of personal experiences; and this has aided much in forming conclusions.

The average man would like to get at the plain, unvarnished facts. He desires to find the truth, both for its own sake, and for its possible uses. If there is even a modicum of virtue in the systematic employment of thought energy, either in behalf of another, or in self-application, for the healing of human woes and ills, the world seriously needs such a re-enforcement, and every lover of his kind would welcome it. If, on the other hand, it has no exact basis, its hollowness should be exposed.

An honest and impartial search for truth for its intrinsic value, in any department, is rarely unprofitable. Many of the scientific treasures that have been unearthed in the past, which have greatly enriched human accomplishment, have been found in unexpected, and even familiar places, where multitudes had almost stumbled over them. This has been true in physical, as well as in social, political, and ethical science. When new truth — new only to human appreciation — has been finally interpreted and introduced, every one wonders that a thing so obviously simple was so long delayed. The apparent slowness, therefore, is not on account of any complexity, but because of general unreadiness.

But truth is, and ever will be, restless until recognized. Each special truth is needed to fill a fitting niche in the greater Unit, and there is discrepancy and incompleteness until it finds its place. When Kepler discovered the law which regulates and adjusts planetary revolution, it was found to be the keystone of an arch of indefinite strength and extent.

Have we in mental therapeutics a great principle, capable of wide application, that is so near that we have looked right through and beyond it? Are there orderly forces in the realm of mind, the utilization of which is more important to mankind than those recently harnessed in the electrical domain?

Admitting that some charlatanism, extravagance, and a spice of disorderly logic have swathed themselves around this new development, it is clearly in the line of legitimate philosophical inquiry, as well as humanitarianism, to find, through impartial research, if it have laws which are of exact definition. We have yet hardly arrived at the threshold of an intelligent understanding of the principles of mental dynamics. We are ever ready to study political, social, moral, and other objective economies exhaustively, but strangely omit that one which is nearest and most vital.

At the present moment, mental, or psycho-therapeutics is almost past that stage of flippant criticism, misapprehension, and prejudice through which all new advances have to make their way. This testing, through adverse criticism, and even ridicule, is not altogether to be deplored, nor is it without real use. It renders a needed service in sweeping off extravagances which always attach themselves to new developments. Only by such a fusing can that which is real be purified of its dross. The residuum of truth has inherent vitality. Fires cannot burn it, nor waters quench its living energy. The struggle through which it passes is educational, both to its assailants and defenders.

Theological, social, economic, and ethical systems become gradually softened towards innovators, and finally coalesce, or at least make terms with them; and the therapeutic and materialistic dogmatisms of the past, which have come down to us, will form no exception to the rule. But nothing is bad. One of the most suggestive lessons of synthetic evolution is, that everything has a use in its place and time. Each system forms a terrace or platform from which men may reach higher.

In every discussion accurate definitions are very

important. The broader science of mental and physical healing, through the potencies of mind, is not distinctively Christian Science, or Faith Healing, nor is it merely another therapeutic system added to the various "pathies" now extant. The term Christian Science, though often used in a general sense, properly belongs to, and should be identified only with a single school which takes for its exclusive text-book a work entitled "Science and Health," by Mrs. Mary B. G. Eddy; and the Bible as interpreted through it. This statement is made in an impartial spirit, as a matter of definition, and of simple justice to all concerned. The distinctive philosophy known as Faith Cure is also quite different from the normal and broader principles that are in accord with law. Faith Cure, proper, presumes upon special divine interposition in answer to prayer. This must involve a suspension or violation of orderly law. As a matter of fact, owing to the working of subtle mental forces, many remarkable cures take place under its administration, only the *modus operandi* being misunderstood. The third radical distinction, as hinted at above, is, that this new philosophy of life — which in its essence is broad, free, and impersonal — is vastly more than merely a new therapeutic competitor, which will strive for a place among existing systems. Its province is quite distinct, and its healing efficacy is only incidental and expressive. Its motive is compliance with orderly law, and it contains no elements which are magical or supernatural. While believing that there are many objective aids to the interpretation of truth, it recognizes no external authority as located in person or text-book. It is a development from within rather than a system; a life rather than a doctrine; a new consciousness rather than a new philosophy; a spiritual optimism rather than a material or pessimistic realism. Its business is to bring inner ideals into outward actualized expression. It has to do with the intuition as well as the intellect, and it recognizes that the inner and real nature of man is in most intimate relation with the Universal Mind and Wholeness. By sympathetic vibration therewith it may, through consciousness, receive inspiration and strength.

Through various subjective colorings, different minds observe in expressive phenomena, occult or miraculous aspects; but when the Established Order is recognized in its higher ranges, there is nothing which is supernormal, supernatural, or super-reasonable. These shadings are entirely due to the low standpoint of the observer.

Following these partial preliminary definitions, a few of the obstacles and current objections may be noted. Truth is eternally complete, but to human consciousness it is incomplete. But every new development only comes into its abiding-place through friction and misapprehension. What there *is* already occupies all the space, and the new-comer seems to be an intruder. There is "no room in the inn."

The full recognition of mental causation for all outward phenomena will necessitate a re-examination of systems which are dignified by hoary antiquity and eminent respectability. Institutions that have exercised unquestioned authority, that are intrenched behind barriers of intellectual scholasticism, and that possess social and financial supremacy, instinctively feel that their infallibility is called in question. Piles of ponderous, dusty tomes thereby become mere relics of bygone speculation.

But mental causation for physical conditions is in substantial harmony with the highest and best thought of the seers and philosophers, from Plato down to the present time.

Popular prejudice against mental- or psycho-therapeutics arises largely from an inability to cognize the factors involved. Prevailing materialism makes it logical to rely upon that which appeals to the senses. A majority are color-blind to the highest order of forces, and forget that even in the external world it is not matter, but the immaterial energy which moulds it, that produces all phenomena. Occidental civilization in its general trend is distinctly external, almost superficial.

Popular misapprehension also arises from the mystical, technical, or dogmatic presentation of principles which, though inherently simple, are made to appear unreasonable, and sometimes fanatical. Although there is truth above reason, as ordinarily defined, there is none against reason. There is spiritual as well as intellectual common-sense. Extreme statements, even if ideally true, should not be popularly presented in unqualified form, for they lead to unnecessary antagonism.

Sensational and exaggerated accounts of occasional failures in the new practice are spread broadcast by the daily press, while it is rare that any allusion is made to the numerous cures of those who had previously exhausted the "regular" systems. While thousands of young and robust people die under conventional treatment every week, after short illnesses, no question is raised nor criticism made. If in the beaten track, everything is taken for granted. Every one has the right to "pass out," if he will only do so according to regulation.

But failures do occur in mental practice. No matter how perfect a principle may be, it cannot have perfect application because of local limitations. The imperfection of the practitioner, and the lack of receptivity in the patient — to say nothing of surrounding antagonistic thought — are limitations.

Many expect sudden and magical improvement, and therefore, being disappointed, abandon the treatment before a sufficient period has elapsed for the legitimate results to appear. Some are unconsciously non-receptive because of a mental resolution that nothing shall in the least disturb their favorite creed, opinion, or philosophy. In this way their door is unwittingly barred against their own improvement. Some are harboring secret sin, or giving place to currents of thought colored with selfishness, envy, sensuality, jealousy, or avarice; and, though unaware of the difficulty, their minds are closed against the truth which could set them free. That which is distorted cannot in a moment become symmetrical, and even after thorough thought reconstruction the body cannot at once fully conform and change its expression. Limitations can be overcome, but patient effort is required. It is easy to float with the tide, but to break away from environment demands courage and persistence. The all-enveloping thought currents are powerful. Even the Great Exemplar in some places "could not do many mighty works" because of prevailing unbelief.

A prevalent distrust of mental practitioners on account of a lack of conventional study, especially in pathology, is quite natural. But sometimes "weak things" confound those which are mighty. A study of pathology is a pursuit of abnormity. If mind be the field of operation, it is evident that it must be kept pure, clean, and entirely free from disorderly and diseased pictures. Thoughts, ideals, and suggestions must all be of health, perfection, and harmony. It is therefore plain that, from the standpoint of mental causation, pathological research would not only be useless, but perhaps harmful. The uniform and only diagnosis of the mental healer must be *health*, HEALTH, HEALTH, really, potentially, and inwardly, even though not yet outwardly actualized. He may divine the particular location of the lack of wholeness, but all the more he sees and emphasizes the potential and inner perfection of that special part or organ. The patient at length comes into at-one-ment. Thoughts are outlines to be filled in; and they must be drawn upon the lines of the pure, the true, and the beautiful.

There is also some prejudice because a majority of the exponents of mental science belong to the so-called "weaker sex." Generally men are more intellectual, though less intuitive, than women, and they are also much more strongly bound in scholastic and traditional grooves and systems. This is distinctively the woman's age; and what is more natural than that the rosy dawn of new esoteric truth should be soonest recognized by her more sensitive spiritual vision?

If mental and physical deviation from the normal were steadily diminishing under conventional applications, there would be little reason for a search for anything better. On the contrary, we find that disorders are steadily growing more subtle and complex. Specialists grow more numerous, and each finds just what he looks for. Physicians are increasing in number in much greater proportion than the population, and diseases and remedies multiply. The more human abnormity is held up and analyzed, the more its various phases and complications manifest themselves. As our civilization recedes from Nature, and artificialism in all directions grows more pronounced, we become hyper-sensitive to discord and morbidity. Insanity, insomnia, and nervous degeneration are increasingly prevalent; and even the physical senses, more than ever before, require artificial aids and props. We are depending upon the Without rather than the Within.

Why expect new advances in electricity and the physical sciences, and at the same time, in a far more important realm, look for nothing better than the universal discord and disorder of the past?

While dealing with obstacles and objections, we may note an inquiry which is often made, which is, If spiritual development tends towards physical harmony, why do we often see those of beautiful and lovable character in conditions of chronic invalidism? Often because of a false theology, which teaches them that God sends trouble, and that it is their duty to accept and bear it. Again, because of a belief that suffering and disease are normal, therefore irremediable. One may be a model in character and conduct, and still entirely fail to mentally assert a rightful rule over his physical organism. "As a man thinketh in his heart so is he." We often unwittingly create our own limitations, and then with the best of intentions actually consecrate them.

Another assumption is often made that there is a correspondence between food and drugs. Not so. One is normal, the other abnormal; one contains nourishment, the other does not; one furnishes natural material for the life-forces to grasp and build up, the other proposes to alter and correct the life-forces themselves. Can they ever be wrong? They are the divine energy in humanity, and never need correction. This vital force, being immutably accurate, only requires that we remove obstructions and come into at-one-ment with it, in order that it may have free course. No drug by mysterious magic can remove penalty. Food meets a normal demand, not to add more life, but to furnish material for life's outward expression.

Still another question is sometimes put forth, and is often regarded as a poser: What about broken bones? Simply, one should get the best surgeon that is available. Surgery is an exact science, in which there has been great advances in the recent past. The surgeon is a mechanical expert who with skill adjusts the parts, and then the divine recuperative forces vitalize the work. Without these forces all the surgeons in the world could not heal the smallest cut. But, as will be shown later, these forces can be greatly augmented. Aside from accidents, however, there are many "operations" undertaken which in reality are unwise, unnecessary, and hazardous.

We may anticipate one other question that is often asked, which is, In the event of acute and very serious illness, would you rely upon mental forces alone? Under present conditions, no. In desperate cases, where there has been no previous higher mental growth or development, a little time may be necessary. But seeming limitation is entirely local, and does not inhere in the principle itself. Without admitting any healing potency, *per se*, in the drug, general belief and acceptance have clothed it with some power, both in the conscious and sub-conscious mind. Even a bread-pill, through personal belief, may prove a powerful cathartic; but nothing less than general belief would insure uniform results. Confidence in the remedy and the physician, and the psychological influence of the latter, with surrounding beliefs and acceptances in the thought atmosphere, all together form an important element. It is often admitted that the prescriptions of a practitioner for whom the patient has an aversion, or even a lack of confidence, have little or no power for good. Until there is a more general growth of reliance upon super-sensuous forces, their field will mainly be among those ills which are not immediately of a very decisive nature. This is expedient, not from any fault of the law, but from prevailing materialism, unintelligent criticism, and unjust intolerance. But acute disorder can be approached from both sides; and there is no incongruity in extreme cases in the employment of both material and mental aid, until public opinion has become softened and educated. But absolute prevention, rather than any kind of cure, is the ideal for the future. When men generally learn to make a scientific application of the divine energies that are stored up within, — through the creative power of thought, — the mental healer will be as thoroughly superfluous as the dispenser of drugs. Having touched upon definitions, obstacles, and objections, we may now come to basic principles.

If primary causes for mental and physical ills are resident in the clay of the body, there is no warrant whatever for healing through mind. If, on the other hand, causative forces are located in the mental realm, there is no logical basis, *per se*, for anything else.

We are in bondage to the seen, and constantly speak of mere occasions as causes. We conventionally say that the draft caused the cold, the contagion or malaria the fever, or the unfriendly microbe the disease. These are occasions, but not causes. The latter, in every case, is in the subjective condition — sometimes called susceptibility. Occasions are always without; causes within. This is proved by unlike results in different individuals. Ten persons sit in the same draft, are exposed to the same contagion or malaria, or swallow the same microbes. Some will suffer, and perhaps die, while the others go scot-free. This shows that occasions are only opportunities. Owing to general low development, opportunities must often be avoided, but they never become causes. All visible phenomena are symptoms and effects. They have something back of them. To hold bullets and shells responsible for the carnage of a battle, rather than passion and antagonism, is a fair illustration. Before citing specific proofs of mental causation, let us briefly consider the nature of man.

What is he? that is, what is the ego? Is he a bundle of living matter, having a diluted something called soul? or is he soul having material expression? Although he has a theological opinion that he *has* a soul, he practically feels that he is *now* body. But he is as much soul as he ever will be. He mistakes, in his consciousness, his own identity, and therefore supposes that he is material in his *being*. This low standpoint surrounds him with self-made limitations, and fills him with a constant soul-hunger. Materialism is his radical mistake.

No man has ever seen his friend or himself. If soul were only a property of bodily organization, there would be no warrant for existence after the laying aside of the form. There is but one real world for any one, and that is his thought world. This should be intelligently constructed. The kingdom of heaven is within, and should be erected upon an exact or scientific basis. Thinking creates its own distinctive environment.

Whether the man or the body be enthroned in the mental realm makes a radical difference. One must rule and the other serve. If the instrument dominate the owner, there is disaster. Inversion is disorderly and destructive. With the man in full command, the body is a graceful complement. If otherwise, it is a tyrant. In the proportion that a spiritual self-consciousness is cultivated, there is a growing sense of command of the visible instrument.

As man truly recognizes himself, assumes the prerogatives of his divine being, and knows that he is a spiritual dynamo, here and now, he wields new forces, and grasps supernal powers and privileges. He comes into at-one-ment with the divine creative principle, and, from a condition of vassalage, finds himself a prince of the realm.

By virtue of his subjective transformation, he establishes new relations with the external domain, and then laws and conditions pay him tribute instead of exacting it. He becomes a spiritual alchemist, and through the alembic of the divinity awakened within him is able to transmute the seeming "common and unclean" into the pure, the ideal, and the God-like. He divines the beneficence of the cosmical economy, and adjusts himself to it. Enlisting all law in his behalf, through an understanding of, and compliance with, its methods, he uses it as though it were his own. He thus re-enforces himself with supernal and cosmic energy by conforming to divine plans and specifications.

The visible form is the stereotype plate, cast from the fused, immaterial composition of past mental states. Matter, whether erected into vegetal, animal, or human configurations, is moulded and qualified by the soul-forging which goes on within. It is plastic material, having no character of its own; for the identical dust is used over and over again to outwardly express different planes and qualities of life. It is picked up by mind or life, and gradually shaped to perfect conformity.

Material science and *materia medica* deal with forms, symptoms, and results. Materialistic evolution does the same. True evolution is entirely in ascending qualities of mind, and these suitably clothe and express themselves visibly. The fleshly form is only the painted canvas of the artist within, who is always busy in translating subjective unseen energy into visible articulation. Owing to the apparent slowness and wonderful complexity of the process, we fail to note the delicate and perfectly adjusted correspondence.

We may now note some illustrations of the power of concentrated thought or suggestion upon bodily conditions. Mental causation is abundantly proved by the well-known effects of fear, anger, envy, anxiety, and the other passions and emotions upon the physical organism. Acute fear will paralyze the nerve-centres, and sometimes turn the hair white in a single night. A mother's milk can be poisoned by a fit of anger. An eminent writer, Dr. Tuke, enumerates as among the direct products of fear, — insanity, idiocy, paralysis of various muscles and organs, profuse perspiration, cholerina, jaundice, sudden decay of teeth, fatal anæmia, skin diseases, erysipelas, and eczema. Passion, sinful thought, avarice, envy, jealousy, selfishness, all press for external bodily expression. Even false philosophies and limited and untrue concepts of the Deity make their unwholesome influence felt in every bodily tissue. By infallible law mental states are mirrored upon the body; but because the process is gradual and complex, we fail to observe the connection. Mind translates itself into flesh and blood.

What must be the physical result upon humanity of thousands of years of chronic fearing, sinning, selfishness, anxiety, and unnumbered other morbid conditions? These are all the time pulling down the cells and tissues which only divine, harmonious thought can build up. Is it surprising that no one is perfectly healthy? Because of its being common, abnormity is rated as normal, or "natural."

The helpful or depressing influence of mind is present in every function, — throbbing in the heart, breathing in the lungs, and weaving its own quality into nutrition, assimilation, sensation, and motion.

It may be objected that children are not responsible thinkers. But they are little sensitive mirrors, in which surrounding thoughts and conditions are reflected and duplicated.

A conscious fear of any specific disease is not necessary to induce it. The trickling rill of conscious thinking has rendered turbid the whole sub-conscious reservoir. The accumulated strands of the unconscious fear of generations have been twisted into the warp and woof of our mentality, and we are on the plane of reciprocity with disease, regardless of the particular form in which it appears. Our door is open to receive it. What is it? A mental spectre. A kingly tyrant crowned by our own sensuous beliefs. It has exactly the power that we have conferred upon it. We have galvanized it into life. As a negative condition it is existent, but not as a God-created entity.

Perhaps there are no more significant examples of the power of suggestion in history than those experiences known as stigmatization. Like everything else not superficially evident, it has been rated as "supernatural." The term, as most persons are aware, refers to marks, tatoos, or scars branded upon the body, corresponding to the wounds believed to have been inflicted upon Jesus at the Crucifixion. The graphic realism of art, as employed in the Roman

Church, produced vivid mental pictures of the Passion. A crucifix held before the eyes, adored, kissed, and concentrated upon by sensitive and highly wrought natures tended powerfully towards physical out-picturing as a natural result. Such manifestations were denominated miracles.

The first historic example which is beyond a doubt, is that of St. Francis of Assisi (Sept. 15, 1224). While intensely meditating upon the tragedy of Calvary in his cell on Mount Alverno, wounds appeared upon his body. There were five deep scars, those upon the hands and feet having the appearance of nails thrust through, and a severe one in the side which occasionally bled. These facts are attested by his reliable biographers, Thomas of Celano and Bonaventura, and also by Pope Alexander IV., who, with many other witnesses, declare that they had seen them both before and after his death. A similar phenomenon occurred in the next century in the case of St. Catherine of Siena, a sister of the order of St. Dominic. It seems probable that St. Paul's declaration, "I bear in my body the *stigmata* of Jesus," has the same significance; but of this there is no collateral evidence. Beginning with St. Francis, and coming down to the present time, there are about ninety well-authenticated cases of stigmatization on record, of which eighteen were males, and seventy-two were females. Generally the order of infliction was the same as that recorded of the Crucifixion, the first token being a bloody sweat, followed by scars of the thorny crown, then the hand and foot wounds, that of the side being last.

The stigmatization of the nun Veronica Giuliana (1696) was remarkable. She drew upon a paper an outline of the images which she said had been engraved upon her heart. After her death (1727) a *post mortem* made by Professor Gentile and Dr. Bordega revealed in deep outlines the cross, scourge, etc., upon the right side of that organ. Other cases are also recorded of heart-marking when no scars appeared upon the surface. In still others, very severe pains were locally experienced without any marks.

A young woman in Saxony (1820) was subject to stigmatic trance. She appeared as if dead on Good Friday, and revived on Easter Sunday.

The *stigmata* have appeared sometimes in colored circles of various hues, often of blackish gray, and sometimes in rose-colored patches. In many cases the scars, and even the bleeding, would occur on Good Friday, and disappear on the following Easter Sunday. Details might be multiplied. Instances occurring in recent times, minutely recorded, and well known in medical annals, have merely been classed as remarkable or abnormal by conventional science, and thus dismissed. Intelligently to turn such herculean mental forces in the opposite and beneficent direction seems not to have been thought of, because the law of operation was not grasped. Everything strange was thought to be "supernatural," and that was a finality. Stigmatic pains and wounds were superstitiously regarded as special tokens of divine favor. But we now know that to gaze absorbedly upon the placid, beneficent portraiture of the Christ, as represented by some of the modern artistic ideals, would be beautifying and uplifting in the highest degree.

Outcroppings of so-called "miraculous healing" have appeared all through the ages, and still continue at various shrines, and from contact with sacred relics. A notable instance is found in the Bambino (image of the infant Jesus), which is contained in the Church St. Marie in Araceli, Rome. This little bejewelled image is conveyed to the houses of wealthy Roman citizens in cases of dangerous illness, with remarkable results. Numerous cures at Lourdes and Traves, France, are well known and admitted by all who have made any careful investigation. The facts are undoubted, but the philosophy of the process has been mystified and misunderstood.

The possible intensity of mental energy is shown in many of the phenomena of hypnotic suggestion. Red or blistered letters or designs are marked upon the arm of a subject, following the simple tracing of a pencil, or even the finger, under the supposition that it is a hot iron.

The principle of mental causation is widely recognized in an endless variety of phases among barbarous and half-civilized races. Aboriginal tribes are near to nature, and keen in locating causes. Thus, charms, incantations, dances, images, and ceremonies have a wonderful influence for healing. They divert the mind, stimulate the faith, and awaken recuperative forces to action. If baseless superstition can be so efficacious, what is not possible by a judicious use of thought reformation?

But as if to heap up evidence, "Ossa on Pelion," come the latest developments of physical science in confirmation. Recent experiments in the laboratories of psycho-physicists — notably those of Prof. Elmer Gates, recently of the Smithsonian Institute — chemically demonstrate mental causation. In a recent interview he says: —

"Bad and unpleasant feelings create harmful chemical products in the body which are physically injurious. Good, pleasant, benevolent, and cheerful feelings create beneficial chemical products which are physically healthful. These products may be detected by chemical analysis in the perspiration and secretions of the individual. More than forty of the good, and as many of the bad, have been detected. Suppose half a dozen men in a room. One feels depressed, another remorseful, another ill-tempered, another jealous, another cheerful, another benevolent. Samples of their perspiration are placed in the hands of the psycho-physicist. Under his examination they reveal all these emotional conditions distinctly and unmistakably."

Some one may inquire, What about the observance of hygienic law? Man fails to study the laws of his own being, and gives all his attention to external conditions. He critically analyzes everything in the whole cosmos, except the one thing most important, — his own constitution. From the material standpoint, environment seems discouraging, and even hopeless. So soon as one hostile element is vanquished, another, yet more subtle, is found concealed in ambush behind it.

Bacteriology has let loose an infinite host of insidious enemies which threaten us at every vulnerable point. Even nature is interpreted as adverse, and the very elements are thought to be in hostile combination against poor humanity. Human pride flatters itself that the causes of its ills are outside. It would avoid responsibility. Under the influence of an effeminate artificialism, which is really abnormal, we unwittingly link deadly qualities to air, water, climate, fog, heat, cold, cloud, rain, or sunshine, when by concordant vibration on our part they would be friendly and normal. There is no mistake in the cosmic plan. Hygiene builds a great dam to stay the current of threatening evils; but in vain, for it rises and soon flows over. It is built higher, and the leaks patched; but it yields, for its foundation is upon the quicksand.

But it will be urged that hygienic observance is rational, and that experience indorses and enforces compliance with it. Must we not destroy adverse bacteria, and maintain barriers against contagions and epidemics? It is freely admitted that for the present we must observe many of the limitations to which we, and those before us, have yielded allegiance, or as a community suffer the penalties. But the ideal to develop is that of an inner and spiritual armor, as scientific as it is spiritual, that will become an impenetrable shield. The creative forces of thought must be brought under intelligent control, until emancipation from the distortions of sense-perception is accomplished.

Let us now briefly touch upon the practical application of the healing-power of one mind as exerted upon another. The fact that thought vibrations can be projected, and strike unisons in another mind, has been scientifically demonstrated, and few will deny it. Certain persons of highly trained and concentrative power can gradually induce a new quality of consciousness in the receptive mentality of others. A degree of passivity and harmony of purpose in the recipient is necessary. Soon the invalid begins to think differently of himself. The better thought seems to be entirely his own; but in reality he has been assisted. There is no hypnotic imposition, but only the calm, concentrated working of two minds for one result. A re-enforcement, or thought ministration, is sent to where it is most needed. The healer has no power in his own personality; but his projected ideal, for which he is only a kind of channel, is the working force. With a clear and clean mind of his own, he looks through and beyond the adverse external appearances of the other, striving to awaken a perfect ideal that may at length be brought into expression. He penetrates to where influences are radiated outwards. Gradually, visible sequence and manifestation fall into line.

The patient is like a discordant instrument which needs tuning. A successful healer must be an overflowing fountain of love and good-will. He makes ideal conditions present. The patient's mental background is like a sensitive plate, upon which will gradually appear outlines of health and harmony as positively presented.

This is no mere narrow professionalism. All can exert healing influence in some degree. Every one should project thought-ministrations of wholesome and perfect ideals into other minds. We are thinking, not for ourselves, but for the world. Thoughts are positive forces. Even their unconscious vibrations go out in never-ending waves; but when *consciously* projected with an aim, their impact upon the resonant strings of other minds stirs them to action. Every ego is a creative centre. Not that he forms anew, but brings something of the Universal into manifestation. Thought energy, so cheaply valued and so aimlessly squandered, can be made infinitely more valuable than material treasures. We make ideals *our own* by *holding* them; and this both actualizes them and gives them to others. Material ownership has but one objective, but a single ideal can be held by thousands. Every owner, instead of consuming it, only makes it richer, and passes it along.

But turning from the influence of one mind upon another, let us briefly consider self-development. Beginning on the lowest plane, what can one do for one's own physical ailments? Granted, as already shown, the wonderful potency of mental pictures, the amazing importance of intelligent and ideal thinking is at once evident. If thought energy be so great and vital, the most important question for each one is, How can I control and direct it? In every mind there are more or less indefinable fears, spectres, imaginings, forebodings, and morbid depressions which we would fain dismiss, but find it impossible. They are the "skeletons in our closets," of whose existence even our most intimate friends are unaware. And now comes the startling knowledge that these mental tenants, besides being generally disagreeable, are actually engaged in pulling down the physical organism. How shall we be rid of them? They cannot be forced out by mere wishing, any more than darkness can be driven from a room. But as light will dissipate darkness, so truth and ideals will displace error. But even in these seeming evils there is a beneficent purpose, when rightly interpreted. They come to goad the consciousness, and make it uncomfortable in the dark, damp basement of its nature, in order that it may be induced to mount to the upper and sunny apartments.

It is the office of pain to disengage the tendrils of our being from negative and material conditions, otherwise we might always remain, and finally become, reconciled to sin and abnormity. The established order wisely provides penalty for arrested development; and when understood it is educational. Conformity to law is the antidote. Thought must be trained and ideals held until they become embodied and expressed. An ideal is a present possession, and by immutable law it seeks to out-picture and actualize itself visibly. Let us illustrate in a simple and practical manner.

Suppose that physical sensation says to one, "You are ill," or "You are very weak." Acquiescence on his part, and that of his friends, is a surrender to the body, a positive servitude. He is no less a vassal because the condition is so common. He should rather turn the thought energy most intensely in the opposite direction. Let him reply mentally, with firm emphasis, "I" (the real ego) "am well." "I am strong." "I am whole." "I am soul." "I rule the body." "I vibrate in unison with the Universal Strength, and open my whole nature to it." Let him repeat and affirm these and similar ideals, even if at first mechanically, and they will gradually *change his consciousness concerning himself*. He thus triumphs over animal sensation, and assumes the rule of his own rightful kingdom. The principle has endless forms of application which will suggest themselves. Can one do this thoroughly and successfully the first time? Assuredly not. As well ask if a child who is just learning the alphabet can read a poem. All development is a growth. The affirming of ideals should, therefore, begin months before the time of their seeming necessity.

One's ideals are his most intimate companions. They impress their quality upon him far more deeply than do personal friends. Shall they be health, harmony, happiness, love, purity, and strength; or disorder, inharmony, malice, fear, sensuality, and weakness? Choose ye, and they will install themselves in the consciousness. We *adopt* them, and they *mould* us.

As a rule, we mentally dwell upon the plane of physical sensation. But such a slavery can be gradually overcome if we will heed the law and firmly hold the ideal.

The great reservoir of sub-conscious mind automatically impresses its quality upon the physical organism. But its contents can be gradually changed by the introduction of the little rill of conscious thought of a different kind.

Let us briefly outline a system which, if persistently followed, will repay one an hundred-fold. Take some available hour each day, and quietly and restfully be alone in the silence. Bar out all current events, anxieties, and sensations, and retire to the inmost sanctuary of soul. Bring in the highest ideals that one wishes embodied, and sit face to face with them. They will increasingly become one's *condition*, and discords will be displaced. Any wakeful hour at night will also serve an excellent purpose. Besides its restorative potency, it will grow to be a veritable mental and spiritual banquet — the most delightful of all the experiences of life. This is idealism, practically and scientifically applied.

Besides the ideals before suggested, there are some that are greater and more purely spiritual in character, which virtually include all other good things that are below them in grade. We venture to hint at a few: I am one with the Eternal Goodness. I am filled with the Universal Spirit. "In Him we live and move and have our being." I project thought vibrations of love to God and all humanity. All is good. I recognize the divine in me as my real ego. I deny the bondage of matter; I am spirit. I rule. I am pure, strong, well — potentially whole. "All things are yours."

Through concentration these healing and uplifting truths are engraven upon the consciousness in a vastly deeper degree than by mere ordinary surface thinking. The individual not only thinks them, but gives himself to them.

The contemplation of pure and elevating works of art, especially a placid and spiritual type of portraiture, is also very helpful as a prolonged suggestive exercise. In the same way visible mottoes, graphic and positively ideal in character, are excellent to dwell upon. Through the medium of the eye, by exposure, their truth becomes photographed upon the deep living consciousness. We become or grow like what we mentally live with. Shall we choose beauty and wholeness, or deformity and disease? We do not desire suffering and *stigmata*, but the true, living, joyful, Christly perfection. The results of a six months' trial of pure scientific mental gymnastics will be both a surprise and a delight. It will greatly enrich life, and increase the power of accomplishment upon every plane. It will be a veritable revelation to victims of insomnia, dyspepsia, nervous prostration, and pessimistic depression, not to mention numerous other mental and physical infelicities. It is an accessible realm to rich and poor. It costs only earnest effort.

Let us now note a few of the more distinctive religious aspects of this higher philosophy of life. Historically, it is easy to see that it is in accord with revelation, and with the purest ideals of all religions.

While rebuking scholastic and dogmatic systems on the one hand, and pseudo-scientific materialism on the other, it vitalizes and makes practical the principles of the Sermon on the Mount. The healing of to-day is the same in kind, though probably not equal in degree, to that of the primitive church. Jesus plainly recognized it as an act within, or a changed consciousness. His definite and repeated explanation was: "Thy faith hath made thee whole." In a pre-eminent degree he could touch the key of that faith, but *it* did the work. Healing is in accord with spiritual law, which is ever uniformly the same under like conditions. As outward and practical attestation, it ought never to have dropped out of the church. The divine commission to preach the gospel and heal the sick includes two different sides of one whole. By what authority is one declared binding through the ages, and the other ignored? Who will assert that God is capricious, so that a boon for one era should be withdrawn from another? "These signs shall follow them that believe." Are such limited to time, race, or location? As ecclesiasticism and materialism crept into the early church, and it became allied with the state, notably in the time of Constantine, and personal ambitions and worldly policies sapped its vitality, spiritual transparency and brotherly love faded out, and with them went the power, or rather the recognition of the power, to heal.

A normal concept of God as Omnipresent Good strongly aids in producing the expression of health. Seeming ills are not God-created entities, but human perversions and reflected images of subjective states.

Both science and dogmatic theology, not yet recognizing the universal beneficence of law, infer that negative or so-called evil tendencies in man may keep on growing indefinitely. Materialism logically leads to pessimism. But the evolutionary trend is forward. As a disciplinary and educational process, evil, which may be defined as distorted thinking, does continue for a while; but it meets with an ever-increasing friction which the divine beneficence has fixed in the established order. Subjective distortions will at length accomplish their educational purpose. One of the great healing forces is the deep intuitive perception that there is no evil — which includes everything that is called bad — as a universal objective principle, but that it is only a name for views through subjective lenses that are colored and abnormal. It is therefore obvious that the highest ideals are normal and true, and that everything less is in a deep sense untrue.

There is a spiritual, as well as a sensuous, chemistry. The most accurate proportion of material substances must be blended to produce a given compound; so a soul-structure, to be symmetrical, must be as carefully composed. Prophets and poets are becoming expert spiritual chemists; and the true elements of the kingdom of heaven — which is subjective harmony — are being scientifically recognized. Just those constituents that are able to satisfy the universal soul-hunger of humanity will be judiciously sought out, and their combination intelligently provided for.

Scientific idealism is the expert alchemist, whose invaluable services are at the command of every earnest soul. Man is a secondary creator, and a boundless quantity of unmanifested good encompasses him on every side. There is a profusion of health, strength, beauty, opulence, harmony, and courage heaped up about him waiting for appropriation. The higher consciousness is the channel through which they may be embodied. Through positive formative thought we gain the title-deeds to invaluable possessions. With the wand of affirmation we project them into expression and actuality. Vitality is pressing in upon us on every side in the attempt to break through our false limitations. There is no loss and no decay, and every perfection stands patiently waiting for our nod of recognition.

The physicist has ever been searching for the great secret of matter, but it ever eludes pursuit. No scalpel will ever penetrate deeply enough to touch it, nor microscope be powerful enough to bring it into the field of vision. O sensuous man! why continue your quest for the "living among the dead"? Why expect to measure the great overflowing universal vitality with your puny balances and chemical tests? And why expect, through material panaceas, to add to the fulness of that Life which is already universal and omnipresent? Through the magic of your own subjective beliefs and imaginings, sensuous agencies may seem to temporarily serve you, but they can add no new vitality, for they have none. But life is all around us, ready to flow into the manifestation of the sons of God. Truth is everywhere waiting to spring forth into expressive embodiment. Paul was not merely a religionist, but a scientific idealist, when he declared, "All things are yours." As man comes into an intelligent understanding of his equipment of creative power, he will grasp the sceptre of his supersensuous sonship and kingship. So far as he has been faithful over a few things, he will become ruler over many. By faith he will be able to remove mountains of doubt and fear, and cast them into the sea of oblivion. Through a knowledge of being, he will subdue kingdoms and work righteousness.

THE UNITY OF DIVERSITY.

THE inspirational truth which is permeating modern thought is the essential inter-relation of all things. The negative conditions which are so widely prevalent in human consciousness are largely due to the lack of a discriminating sense of the numberless lines of mutual relationship. Emerson voiced this sentiment in the simple words: —

> "All are needed by each one;
> Nothing is fair or good alone."

The law of unselfishness is so fundamental that it is written everywhere. Every leaf, twig, and branch inform us of dependence and interdependence; and every organ of the physical body works unceasingly, more for its neighbors than itself. Reciprocity is the all-prevailing order. In all the varied phenomena of mind and matter nothing stands alone. Selfishness, which is the negative of this universal positive, may be said to be the mainspring of all the woes of humanity.

One Life permeates all things, and there is no corner of the universe too remote to feel its heart-throb. But in the world consciousness of the past, division has been the universal experience. All through the ages there has been a sharp boundary line drawn between the realm of Nature and Spirit. The two have been regarded, not only as thoroughly separated, but as antagonistic. The old partition wall is now decaying and crumbling in human consciousness, and that is the only place where it ever had existence. It is now seen that the natural is spiritual, and the spiritual, natural. There is but one.

The view of the past has been only a view of a part, and hence the world has been filled with the hunger of incompleteness. Life has been incomplete; health has been incomplete; religion, ethics, and sociology have been incomplete. But more disastrous than all else — to the false sense of the world — God has been incomplete. Though holding to a theory of his infinitude and perfection, he has practically, as presented to the human mind, been capricious and changeable. He has been a reflection of the beholder, faithful to the likeness, though seen through a telescope, and indefinitely magnified. Like the object in the lens, though enlarged, he has not been whole. There has been another power almost his equal warring against him. He was, therefore, practically partial. Only occasional seers, scattered along the ages, have had the clearness of vision to get a glimpse of the universal completeness of the Good. Materialism has been so dense and controlling, that it would almost require visible cords, running from everything to everything, to teach men universal relationship.

The sense of selfishness, or separation, manifests itself in an ever-present antagonism. Society is divided into fragments, and each thinks its interest is diverse from all the others. His supreme concern is for his nation, state, sect, section, profession, trade, clique, family, and, most of all, himself. To him the good of each is separate from the general good, and his rise would even be promoted by another's fall. That all are factors in a grander unity, and all dependent and interdependent, is hardly understood. Paul's lesson in regard to the organs of the human body is truly scientific, even though unappreciated. Diversity of interest is only a seeming.

In the general non-recognition of the unity of life the world struggles and suffers. Every man views his own life as a thing by itself; and this concept closes him against the influx of the Universal. But his little pool can only be filled and purified by the sweep of the tides of the great ocean of vitality by which he is unconsciously surrounded. He is virtually isolated from the electric current which flows from the general " power-house." His constant sense of incompleteness erects barriers in front of him whichever way he may face. His God is hardly more complete than himself, only built upon a grander scale. He lives in the ever-abiding *lack* of something. Health, wealth, power, knowledge, happiness — everything, depends upon the ability to recognize the universal completeness. Whatever is held in the individual consciousness is in the deepest sense present and real. Subjective conditions are the lens through which the world is seen; and they give it their own color, tone, and quality. We gain all good things to the degree that consciousness brings them into our possession. He who refuses to harbor or dwell upon incompleteness has his vision opened to eternal wholeness.

We live in the vapid, debilitating atmosphere of tradition, measuring ourselves among ourselves, instead of rising to ideal, manly stature by opening our souls to the exuberant overflow of the divine Fountain. Turning our backs upon our heritage as children of God, we anxiously try to prop up our little detached life by weak and sensuous artifices. Life is already complete in the Universal Life; but, being blind to the sunny horizon above us, we remain in the dim light of a dungeon, grasping at shadows.

Science and religion have divided the world in twain, misunderstanding and opposing each other; each as incomplete as a hemisphere without its counterpart. Religion has proposed to cure the souls of men, but has practically assumed that they are *now* bodies. It recognizes an airy and unsubstantial thing called a "soul," which is susceptible of a legalized salvation for the future. But men need both a present and a scientific salvation — one that is normal rather than "supernatural." Science, on the other hand, has declared that everything beyond the sensuous is a necessarily unscientific. Its gaze has been downward; fixed upon dead, opaque matter. But both science and religion are awaking from their long dream of division and incompleteness, and each, with the instinct of newly discovered relatives, is reaching out for its counterpart.

The supernatural has long been fenced off in an exterior realm, beyond the reign of orderly law, and its distance and strangeness have made it weird and unattractive. Thus the beauty, perfection, and roundness of the sphere of Unity have had a fragmentary and unsymmetrical appearance. Consciousness limits the boundary of the human outlook, and it must be uplifted — born again — before it can mount above the fogs and mists of materialistic negation into the pure azure of the real and spiritual.

No man can change the objective order of things, but the beauty and strength of his own life depend upon his recognition of his intimate relationship to the Universal. Feeling himself to occupy a definite place in the great evolutionary scale, he should advance voluntarily, and escape the friction which otherwise will be his when pushed from behind. When he feels the electric chords through which vitality can come to him converging in his own soul, he grows in power as rapidly as his consciousness

THE UNITY OF DIVERSITY. 153

can expand. He is the creator of his own subjective world, and through its outward lines of relationship colors and transforms the objective realm into correspondence. He chooses his own residence, taking up his abode behind prison-bars, amidst discord and negation, or building within the realm of harmony and orderly relationship. So long as he recognizes different centres of gravity he is rent by their opposing forces. As God becomes to him the Within and the Without, the All in All, the Beginning and the Ending, there comes a sense of the completeness of unity.

Disconnection from relationship manifests itself in leanness and disease. A limited self-consciousness is a barrier which must be broken through before the broad range of *freedom* is attainable. As finited souls we cannot place ourselves outside of the "Oversoul;" but what is impossible in reality is possible in consciousness.

Love is the attractive force which clasps each soul in the universal embrace. Every message of ministry brings back a response of equal intensity. Life is a constant giving and receiving. If we would be sharers of the boundless profusion of the good that is waiting for room to bestow itself, we must plunge into its great current, and become one with it.

The world of sense contains no fountain of life. Humanity is "cumbered with much serving." It wears itself out in a weary search for the essential good in the dry and barren shell of the external, where dwells no vitality. Man is hungering for more life, and yet tries to satisfy his cravings with husks. He must lift up his eyes to behold all vital truth as one and universal, and open his portals for an inflow of its nourishment.

The seeming hard and adverse conditions of the present plane of existence crowd the great completeness out of consciousness. Disappointment, struggle, suffering, and death are ever-present clouds in our horizon. It seems impossible to reconcile their dark lowering with the beneficence of universal law. To the eye of sense the world has no cohesion, and is divided against itself. Disease, cruelty, fear, evil, and mortality hold high carnival, and no deliverance or exemption is visible. We wonder at the seething strife and turmoil which neither conventional religion nor philosophy has explained or assuaged. In deep despair, the racial consciousness, shruken by ages of fear and limitation, has accepted the worst, and concluded that all this agony is normal and irredeemable.

But the kingdom of heaven "cometh not with observation." Looking beneath the turbid and restless waves of this great sea of human experience, we sound its depths, and behold a "great calm." As dark shadows flee before the advent of the "king of day," so the negation of evil dissolves before the rising sun of truth. Mounting the hills to the standpoint of the real, the horizon is clear, and the fulness of life is seen, bursting all material limitations. Oneness in diversity is made plain, and the natural and supernatural melt into each other.

The golden key which is unlocking and bringing to light hitherto dark recesses is the understanding and application of law. Only by its magic has unbounded chaos been transformed into harmonious unity. As we interpret the operative laws of the divine life, we become not only its recipients, but its reflectors and distributers. The nightmare of evil and mortality is lifted, and we walk in the clear light of the real. The wilderness of unshapely fragments which so long filled our gaze, by a kaleidoscopic transformation not only come together, but exactly fit each other.

The world is full of those who see but a single side of truth. This distorts all proportion, and puts out of view the grand and perfect unitary sphere. The boundaries of sect, system, and party not only limit truth, but sever it. Vision is narrowed and focalized upon its immediate possessions, and it soon becomes incapable of seeing anything else.

Paul declares: "All things are yours." We enter into their possession through consciousness. If we fail to receive the great heritage bequeathed to the offspring of the Infinite, the fault is only our own.

THE DYNAMICS OF MIND.

In the light of recent psychical demonstrations, it has been said that thoughts are things; but perhaps a more exact statement would be that they are forces.

In physical science the present trend of teaching is distinctly from the former accepted atomic basis, which included the solidity and potency of matter, towards a hypothesis in which energy is regarded as the underlying principle of all phenomena. Thus the atom, which has never been discovered, and is not likely to be, is no longer recognized as the real unit in the physical economy, energy being now accepted as the primal starting-point.

Manifestations to our senses, which we call light, heat, and sound, are only differentiated modes of vibratory force. Primal energy, unitary in its essence, and always conserved in the aggregate, takes on, to us, one of several qualitative appearances, according to the form of its waves, or rather, perhaps, the rapidity of its vibrations. Under certain circumstances, and through the action of laws yet imperfectly understood, these various modes of manifestation are interchangeably transformed in constant but variable repetition.

THE DYNAMICS OF MIND.

Modern science has accepted the conclusion that vibration is a universal law; and the recognition of this fact is the key which is unlocking mysteries and solving phenomena hitherto unexplainable. It has furnished an all-comprehensive working hypothesis. Beginning with an inter-molecular rhythm of inconceivable rapidity in all bodies, even those that appear to be solid and at rest, its domain of wave-movements extends through all space, and its impulses are coursing in every conceivable direction. They are ceaseless and endless. The cosmos may truly be said to be "all of a quiver."

The basic medium of these innumerable wavy motions is undoubtedly the universal ether, the nature of which can only be dimly conjectured through its multiform manifestations. Who can say that this is not the boundless common meeting-ground between the spiritual and the material? Unaccountably enough, the myriads of vibrations of different kinds and velocities that are sweeping through space do not appear to disturb or neutralize each other in the least. There is a clear path for all.

These late developments in physical science, which in the above statement have only been hinted at in the most general terms, carry with them necessary inferences and correlations, the scope of which can yet hardly be imagined. The dematerialization, or perhaps what may even be called the spiritualization of physics, as a science, is one of the marked logical tendencies. There is also a growing demonstration and conviction of thè deceptive and utterly unreliable nature of sensuous appearances. Science, before finally accepting any proposition as proven, has always insisted upon material and mathematical demonstration. This is well in its place, but is not all; in fact, it is only the lower and cruder side.

Matter, as formerly regarded, seems to be consciously melting into mind or spirit. It is no longer inert or dead, but instinct with life. Its transformations are ceaseless and mysterious. Can any one explain just how and why a visible solid can take the form of an invisible gas, and *vice versa*?

The theoretical boundary line between the immaterial and the material is getting very faint, if not actually disappearing. Let us drop our crude, childish materialism, and rise easily and reasonably to the grand conception that differentiated forces are being traced back, even through the methods of the physicist, to the *One Primal Energy* — INFINITE MIND. The veils which in our infantile development we have hung around external nature are growing so attenuated that we can almost discern with unaided vision the active operation of Supreme Intelligence, Goodness, and Beneficence.

All profound discernment and analogy lead back to the grand fundamental premise that, behind all manifestations, energy is One, that it is an Intelligent Energy, and is therefore Omnipresent Mind. Monism, or the inherent unity of all things, is the growing inspiration of science. It is thereby confirming the impressions already received through the delicate vision of the unfolded interior faculties. Paul's immortal aphorism, that "in him we live and move and have our being," has waited long for scientific indorsement, but it is apparently soon to be realized. We behold the universe as soulful, and not mechanical. This is no ancient superstitious pantheism resurrected. Rather, the Deity is infinitely honored as compared with any and all past human concepts.

If all energy, in its last analysis, be Intelligent Mind, and vibration the universal method, we may reasonably infer that human mind or volition, being in and a part of the whole, should form no exception in the working plan of its orderly activities. If essential, potential, and ideal man be the "offspring," "image," and manifester of God, nothing unlike it could be normal. As the former ideals of a Deity, localized, personified, changeable, and in every way unconsciously limited, are slowly replaced by the transcendent ideal of the unconditioned "All in All," the interrelation of all things to and in God is being grasped. When man refines, enlarges, and elevates his consciousness of Divinity, he does the same for his own deeper and generic spiritual nature, which, though temporarily obscured, is in reality himself.

160 STUDIES IN THE THOUGHT WORLD.

If God be spirit, man, his reflection and likeness, must also be spirit, and not dust. By a traditional and distorted self-consciousness he has thought himself to be a poor, sinful, *material* being; and the formative power of his mental specification has externally actualized his model. He *is* mind or spirit; but his physical expression, which should be of ideal quality, out-pictures his perverted estimate of himself. Not recognizing his true being, he has drawn a mistaken outline, and then naturally filled it out. He has thus unwittingly hidden his own potential and divine forces, though they are still within. The mirror of false consciousness has reflected a doleful image which he has seriously taken for himself.

The purer and higher trend of science is characterized by a gradual refinement and immateriality. The laboratory should become a sanctuary, for in it are gained glimpses of the Eternal. Man himself is being more truly interpreted as the highest expression of divinity. He is a concrete manifestation of the One Mind, finited, but with unlimited possibilities. He is inconceivably great, though ignorantly unaware of it. But a significant indication of his growing consciousness of the possession of supernal power is found in the recent discovery of the dynamic and formative potency of his thought. The Infinite Uncreate is the primal and universal energy, but man is its embodier and manifester. His mental forces cannot create *de novo*, but they can mould, utilize, and express. The unfolded soul having developed a self-consciousness of its transcendent power, intelligently sends out its own vibrations from its own centre. Conforming to the divine plan and chord, it becomes a reflection, or secondary radiator, of rhythms which are concordant with the Original.

We are logically led to the conclusion that the recent recognition of the potency and utility of the projective vibration of thought is an unprecedented and immense step in scientific achievement, human unfoldment, and spiritual evolution. Man is finding his rightful dominant place in nature, in the arcana of soul force and expression, and in his relation to the Infinite.

Before considering specifically the dynamic relations between mind and mind, it may be well to note briefly these relations as they exist between a human mind and its physical counterpart. Man is mind; and this statement implies that the physical organism is not man, but only his visible index or expression. To attempt to prove this is like demonstrating an axiom; but yet mankind at large indicate by their action that they do not practically believe it. Nine-tenths of the care, labor, and attention of the world are bestowed upon the body and its gratification, or upon those subordinate mental powers, the product of which will command the greatest commercial value. Most of the prevailing systems of education, so called, have the same end more or less directly in view.

The trained intellect, including not only technical and professional attainment, but also the powers of literary, poetic, and dramatic ability, eloquence, and wit, are largely rated and valued on an economic and material basis. To train, control, and uplift the mind, and develop its higher faculties for its own sake and that of others, is not common. The world is still endeavoring to "live by bread alone."

Prevailing systems of philosophy, science, theology, therapeutics, sociology, and charity, including Darwinian evolution, all proceed upon the general hypothesis that man is intrinsically a *material* being. So considered he has an attenuated quality called a soul, dependent upon fleshly brain-cells.

The "fall," not historic, but continuous, is from the ideal, potential, and inmostly actual, into the external of appearances; and this comprises the Adamic consciousness. Men cling to the sensuous Eden until they are startled and driven from it by the loud calling of the divine voice within. The beneficent expulsion from that Eden, and the succeeding necessary restlessness, furnish the true and only impetus for voluntary moral and spiritual evolution. The world is still largely peopled with Adams who practically believe that they are made of red earth or dust.

Is man to grasp, mould, and rule that little portion of visible matter that he has temporarily taken on, and which has been often before used to express and embody other qualities of life, or must he believe himself in bondage to it? Shall the shadow, even though real as a shadow, dominate the substance? Not forever, even in what is called this life. So soon as man recognizes the fact that he is a mental and spiritual dynamo, he will no longer remain a vassal in his own legitimate kingdom.

A dominant vibration in the thought atmosphere is able to arouse a nation or a continent. Great minds, as well as those of less development, are submerged and swept along by it. Crusades, reformations, revolutions, and reforms furnish numberless illustrations of psychic upheaval and contagion. Through sympathetic vibration a vast number of responsive mental strings are stirred into action. As the rhythmical step of a regiment will powerfully shake a strong bridge, so the concerted energy of mind will generate tidal waves of tremendous import. The result is not merely from a contemporaneous logical process, carried on respectively by many individuals, but from a great immaterial gulf-stream, deep and mighty, though silent and unconscious.

Mind, as a *force*, is no more unintelligible or unthinkable than other vibrations of unseen energy. And here lies the tremendous significance of the new psychology or recognition of soul-force. Till recently conventional science, as taught in all accepted text-books, recognized no extension of the dynamics of thought beyond the confines of the physical organism. The mind, with feeble domination, through nerve channels, could transmit its orders to different parts of its visible counterpart, but it was not believed that it could go one inch beyond that limit. Any suggestion that telepathy, or thought transference, could take place at a distance of a thousand miles, or even one mile, would have been pronounced impossible.

We shall waste no time in the mere attempt to prove the fact that thought is and can be projected through space, both consciously and unconsciously. No well-informed individual who has given any adequate attention to the subject now questions it. Scores of pages might be filled with examples, now on record, which are entirely beyond collusion or coincidence. Every one of thousands of hypnotic experiences proves it, and every case of healing through mental treatment attests it. There is no fact in physical science better assured.

And how has the world received this transcendent truth which is transforming in its potency, all-inclusive in its sequences, and divine in its possibilities? Very much as it would a new *curio* or an ingenious toy. The institutional psychologist fondles it, turns it over, weighs and measures its properties in his laboratory, speculates *about* it, and makes a profession of it. But the last thing to be thought of is to make it useful to mankind. That would be unprofessional. To harness and utilize this force of all forces for the good of humanity would lower it from the select and charmed circle of professional theory and speculation to the broad plane of practical and beneficent agencies.

The average psychical researcher shows much of the same indifference as to any utilization of his favorite principles and pursuit. He is engaged in a never-ending search for phenomena. He will strain his investigative powers, and burn midnight oil, in testing, comparing, and recording curious manifestations, and in interpreting their methods and laws; but as to their practical application in ethical culture, therapeutic potency, or spiritual unfoldment; he is as innocent as a child. It has not occurred to him. These reflections are made in no impatient spirit as applied to individuals, but rather to show the negative character of systems of thought into which we have allowed ourselves to become crystallized. How much freedom, originality, and progress would at once be manifest if the fear of being called unprofessional and unconventional, which now holds men in bondage, could be eliminated!

Besides the classes already noted, there are many excellent people, lovely in character and pure in motive, whose temperamental fondness for the mystical leads them to seek visions, dream dreams, and to cultivate an order of phenomena more dramatic than profitable. Abstract truth and vivid demonstration are well, but the world is hungering for their application to its woes.

If we have gained some knowledge of the laws which govern a force inconceivably grander and higher than electricity, may we not dismiss undue sensitiveness as to deviations from traditional scholasticism, and for the sake of humanity step out of the ruts which have been grooved by the schoolmen of the darker and narrower past? All great advances in their earlier aspects have been rated as irrational innovations.

Regarding the fundamental basis of psycho-dynamics, not only as admitted, but overwhelmingly proven, let us now concisely sum up a few of the results which logically should be realized. They are of stupendous significance; but, surrounded as we are by the blank walls of our self-imposed and traditional limitations, we can hardly picture them even to the imagination.

Thoughts being forces, every mind is a creative centre from which rhythms of qualitative energy are going out in all directions. By their impact upon corresponding chords in other minds, these are also swept into active vibration. Throw a pebble into a lake, and the placid surface at once becomes vibrant with a series of ever-widening circles which go out to its utmost boundary. They are never quite lost nor neutralized, though we may be unable to trace them to their final destination. So every soul is the seat of a great centrifugal current, which is generated and set free in the simple process of thinking. This is true — though less in degree — of desultory or aimless thought, as well as of that which is concentrated and projected with definite intent. Every thinker is a battery of positive forces, even though he utter never a word.

The soul — which is the man — is a resonant instrument with innumerable tremulous strings of the most delicate quality. The water in the lake responds to the pebble, but the medium through which thought waves pass is infinitely more subtle and elastic.

What volumes of potential energy are wasted, and far worse, in negative and discordant mental activities! We are not thinking for ourselves, but for the world. With the shuttle of thought in the loom of mind, we are weaving the multi-colored fabric of conditions, and these not merely immaterial, but to be outwardly actualized and manifested. If one in his own soul strikes the discordant notes of anger, envy, avarice, selfishness, or even those seemingly more harmless ones of simple fear, weakness, grief, pessimism, or depression, he is creating and vibrating those conditions far and near, thereby stirring the corresponding chords in other souls into sympathetic activity. The sphere of outward action is limited, while that of thought is boundless. Mere doing makes ephemeral reputation, while quality of thinking determines, or rather *is*, vital character.

Every one's thought images are being constantly

impressed both upon himself and others. His mind is a busy factory where conditions are positively manufactured. He weaves their quality, consciously or unconsciously, into every nerve, muscle, and tissue of his own body. His materialistic thought tethers him in a little circle of limitation, while boundless green fields lie beyond waiting for occupation. His mental pictures of evil, disorder, and disease, photograph themselves not only upon his own mind and body, but upon those of his fellows.

One cannot afford to think much about evil, even for the well-intentioned purpose of its suppression. The true remedy is its displacement. Thought space given to it confers realism, familiarity, and finally dominion. To silence discordant strings in ourselves or others we must vibrate their opposites. To truly sympathize with a friend who is quivering with trouble or sorrow, is not to drop into his rhythm and intensify it, — as is usual, — but to lift his consciousness by striking a higher chord in unison. The road to mental and physical invigoration lies through the dynamics of formative thought. Our way to elevate other lives is also through their creative mental energies.

When the art of projecting thought vibrations on a high plane is systematically cultivated, and the concentrative habit developed, potency for good is increased a hundred-fold. Force is no longer squandered in worse than useless discordant negations, but intelligently conserved in positive vigor and exuberance. Purposeful thought ministration, spiritual and pure in quality, accurately and scientifically projected, like an arrow towards a target, is the great harmonizing and uplifting agency that will transform the world. Vibrations of love, peace, spirituality, health, sanity, and harmony, will be radiated in ever-widening circles, striking responsive unisons that are only waiting for a well-directed concordant impulse.

The dynamics of mind, when generally utilized, will be the sovereign balm that with scientific accuracy will heal all the infelicities of society. It will usher in not only reform, but regeneration. In its copious fulness it will overflow from the altitude of spiritual development, until the subordinate plains of intellectuality, ethics, therapeutics, sociology, economics, and physics, are swept, purified, and uplifted. The highest includes everything below. With the Kingdom of Heaven — which is subjective harmony — first sought, "all these things" will be added.

AUTO-SUGGESTION AND CONCENTRATION.

HAVING considered in a previous paper the law of vibratory forces as operative between soul and soul, a study of its exercise in one's individual economy logically follows. But, while individuated, it is clearly impossible for spiritual development to be selfish, because no limitation can enclose it. Egotism is existent only on the sensuous plane. The higher unfoldment, in the very nature of the case, is an upliftment out of one's narrow, baser selfhood. Ideal soul-development in the individual is a work that concerns all humanity. Effort for the true self and that directly in behalf of others are only two different sides of one process.

It will be recalled that in "The Dynamics of Mind" thought vibrations were presented as unlimited in their scope and potency. But great power is valueless unless it be harnessed and directed. Steam, electricity, and even the abounding waterfalls of nature, signify nothing to man until he intelligently grasps their laws, and, through compliance therewith, commands them. It is a question of concordant vibration. The competent engineer mentally vibrates with his engine or dynamo, and multiplies his accomplishment a thousand-fold, while the ignorant meddler not only does not increase his product, but through an inherent judgment suffers penalty. Everything he employs is good, but there is misplacement.

All true objective energy being primarily divine and normal, there can be no evil forces. Those which seem so wear that aspect to us from our ignorant misdirection. Street-sweepings may be valuable as fertilizing material, and for that purpose are clean, but when misplaced they are unclean to us, though not so in themselves.

But this law of universal goodness is not limited to the material or objective realm. The forces of mind are all beneficent. The skill, patience, and persistence of a thief are excellent, but they are subjectively distorted, or turned into a wrong channel. This doctrine comes from no fine-spun metaphysical distinction, but is basic and vital in its final analysis. There is no "evil" as an objective entity. If there were, the Infinite Intelligence created that which is contrary to himself, his laws and methods; an unthinkable supposition.

Law is both universal and beneficent, but owing to materialistic fogginess the latter has been scantily recognized. Even the pain and penalty which are linked to nonconformity to law are good, not ideally but provisionally as they appear. They rise up as educational monitors. When deeply comprehended, the higher evolutionary philosophy involves an unlimited optimism upon every plane of manifestation.

Ignorance of law rather than inherent depravity is responsible for all the woes of humanity. In proportion as the established order is truly interpreted ills will disappear. Law is not that which is artificially imposed from without, but what is inscribed in man's constitution. The Decalogue, and even the Sermon on the Mount, are woven into the fabric of his being, so that violence to them is harmful to him. His real concern is with what is within. As with the "Prodigal," pain and penalty bring men to themselves; that is, to the deeper, real individuality, which is virtually the "Father's House."

The regal dynamics of man's inner being have been wastefully neglected and squandered, while he has incessantly pursued objective phenomena which are only symptomatic and petty by comparison. Human vibrations have been disorderly and out of rhythm with the cosmic order. This has introduced confusion and chaos. Instead of multiplied power, as in the case of a perfect engine run by a skilful engineer, we have been ignorant meddlers, with disastrous results. Human activity in unison with the divine chords would carry irresistible potency. Such co-operation would enlist infinite forces in our behalf. Limitations would thereby be pushed well nigh out of sight.

AUTO-SUGGESTION AND CONCENTRATION. 173

But to give these transcendent principles more specific application to the subject in hand, we may consider, first, the potency of suggestion or intelligent thought action upon mental and physical conditions and expressions, and, second, their rational working means and methods.

Marked beneficent phenomena have been rather infrequent because powerful concentration has generally been haphazard, unscientific, or superstitious, working in the direction of harm instead of good. Its law having been mistaken, this mighty force has been misused and entirely misinterpreted.

A limited and unconscious employment of the law of mental causation has appeared in the occasional outcropping of "miraculous healing" all through the ages, and still continues at various shrines and holy places, and from contact with sacred relics. Numerous cures at Lourdes and Traves in France are well known and admitted by all who have given the matter any careful investigation. To indulge in any general denial of such manifestations, which have been almost numberless, would indicate either ignorance or a most irrational disbelief of evidence that is practically without limit. The facts are undoubted. It is only the *modus operandi* that has been misinterpreted.

It is strange that the devout Romanist should feel that he honored God less by believing that he worked through the orderly laws of the human mind than by external and disorderly interposition. That quality in man which craves a magical and dramatic divine manifestation rather than one which is intelligible and scientific, is largely responsible for keeping the world in thraldom. How transcendent a Deity whose activities are beautifully regular! Our brethren of the Roman Catholic faith will doubtless gradually approach such a reasonable position. The conservative orthodox Protestant is not much more logical, the main difference being that he dates his "miracles" farther back.

Nothing else would so powerfully hasten the long hoped-for reconciliation between science and religion, as a fuller and deeper interpretation of the established order on its higher planes. Religion must become scientific and reasonable, and science must broaden its vision, and include the immaterial and spiritual realm. By such a consummation both would gain, each being indorsed by its true counterpart.

The possible intensity of the energy of mental states is demonstrated in many of the phenomena of hypnotic suggestion. But this phase cannot now be entered upon in detail.

The power of discordant emotional force to turn the hair suddenly white, to poison the mother's milk, to produce disease, and even death, under various conditions, is too familiar to require mention, but may be noted as sufficient in itself to confirm a principle that receives proof in such innumerable directions. But while the disastrous influence of such discordant emotions as fear, grief, anger, anxiety, and depression for pulling down the physical tissues has long been known merely as a fact, the process has remained uninterpreted, and the positive benefits which would accompany their opposites have been unappreciated or ignored.

Virtue and vice, purity and impurity, spirituality and carnality, confidence and fear, love and hate, joy and grief, all through irrepealable law translate their respective qualities into flesh, blood, bone, and sinew. Every possible qualitative thought energy presses for material expression. But the mixture of unlike forces, including positives neutralized by negatives, results in an interminable complexity of the process; and this, together with its apparent slowness under ordinary conditions, has hidden the law from superficial observation. The subtle shadings of heredity also form another deeply involved element. But perhaps, more than all, prevailing materialism, which views the body as the real basis of man, is responsible for spiritual color-blindness and ignorance.

Having found that thought energy, heretofore so lightly regarded, is a tremendous power for good or evil, physically, mentally, and spiritually, a most vital problem presents itself to every individual. How can I train and control my thinking?

Within the mental chambers of every person there

linger, not only some of those emotions commonly classed as sinful, but also a host of indefinable fears, spectres, imaginings, forebodings, and morbid depressions which we would fain dismiss if we could, but find it impossible. They are tormentors of whose existence even our most intimate friends are unaware. We do not wish to give these intruders shelter, but are unable either to drive them out or to coax them to leave. They vary in every mind, but none are entirely exempt. Sometimes they are so intolerable that almost any price would be paid for their removal. And now, added to all this host of mental disturbances, comes the positive knowledge that they are also working silent destruction in the physical organism. Well may one cry out, "What shall I do to be saved?" Saved from what? From my thoughts; from a mass of distorted mental pictures which seem to be myself; from the only thing in the universe that really can harm me.

But before attempting to show the way of salvation, we may suggest that these seeming antagonists are in the deepest degree beneficent when rightly interpreted. What a paradox! They are in reality the kindly chastisements that come to drive us from our discordant materialism into a higher and spiritual self-consciousness. They make us uncomfortable until we learn their lesson. They are the "consuming fire" which burns up the "wood, hay, and stubble," but leaves the divine individuality — the real

AUTO-SUGGESTION AND CONCENTRATION. 177

self — not only unharmed, but purified. We feel the flames just in the proportion that we think our*selves* to be material rather than spiritual beings. They come to release us from a subjective prison which we have unwittingly built out of self-made materials. We may as well use a plain, old-fashioned term, and call them hell. But this state of consciousness is the most powerful evolutionary pushing force in existence. Nothing less could prevent a peaceful reconciliation with sin and evil.

As a negative answer to the question of the way of salvation from these subjective abominations, it may at first be suggested that no bargain can be made with any objective or historic creed or ordinance for deliverance. Neither can we drive out or will away our unwholesome mental guests. Ten men cannot drive darkness out of a room, but the hand of a child may raise a curtain, and the light will do the work. Displacement is the law. Truth casts out error. How can this be applied? Through the normal use of the divine creative thinking-faculty. But the average man says that he "cannot control and concentrate this energy." Pray, when has he made any systematic effort? He will spend years of time, and no end of effort, to educate himself on the surface, but can hardly afford hours for scientific thought training.

As a rule, thought is diffuse, undirected, and open to all the depressing and discordant material which floats by. It may be compared to an unbroken colt without bit or bridle. But it can be educated and made docile. Auto-suggestion and concentration can be intelligently introduced into every-day life. Through their judicious employment, the ills, spectres, beliefs of evil, and disorders of mind and body, may be crowded out of the consciousness, and finally, as a natural result, vanish from outward expression. Daily psycho-gymnastics is needed, and is as important as physical exercise. There should be intelligent and concentrated self-suggestions, that ideals — like health, harmony, and everything good — are a *present possession;* and this attitude of mind, firmly held, in due time will bring them into outward manifestation. Contrary outward appearances and physical sensations must be held in abeyance. The work is back of these, for they are resultant. The inmost and real is already perfect, but we are unaware of it. When we therefore affirm this fact, and dwell upon it, we have the potential and ideal truth, sensations and surface indications to the contrary notwithstanding. The grandest claims must be made as *already* existent, and held to until outwardly actualized. Such thought energy is not irrational, but reasonable, for it is in accord with law. Until it is creatively used, as indicated, its sublime force is squandered, or worse.

Positive entities like health, harmony, goodness, strength, love, and spirituality, must be installed in the consciousness through the normal formative power of thought. Negatives — which are not entities, but only deficiencies — like weakness, disorder, inharmony, disease, malice, and fear, are to be displaced, to gradually become unfamiliar, and finally and ideally *unreal*. But when positive conditions become a habit, so that a permanent purposeful attitude of mind is attained, cures should become unnecessary, because there will be nothing to cure. The practice of daily mental gymnastics, which would include systematic concentration upon ideals, should begin at once, while one is well, in order to prevent remedial necessities in the future.

Any truly scientific use of the dynamics of thought becomes all-inclusive in its beneficent range. It puts forces into human hands which reach out indefinitely in every direction. It is the golden sceptre that man may grasp and wield over the kingdoms within and around him.

HUMAN EVOLUTION AND THE "FALL."

In the world's comparative chronology it was but yesterday that the evolutionary philosophy was itself evolved in the human consciousness. Only its lower and materialistic aspects have yet been recognized by science, the grander and higher visions being still in reserve. But even the limited progress already made marks the most stupendous new departure of all the ages. We have discovered a set of successive keys, so that doors hitherto impenetrable now swing open and reveal endless vistas. Innumerable facts, manifestations, and principles, that have seemed disjointed and meaningless, are now smoothly gliding into their well-fitting niches. A wilderness of heterogeneity by a dissolving view is transformed into homogenetic and living beauty. A chaos of antagonisms and evils, through the new lens of progressive unfoldment, is found to comprise one great Unity, which is perfectly adjusted in all relations.

To properly discuss a subject of such magnitude within the limits of this paper in any technical manner is obviously impossible. But often a synthetic and suggestive presentation of cardinal principles is more profitable — especially to the average reader — than an array of scholastic detail. We often lose or distort the normal perspective of some department of truth by wandering in an analytical maze, and so fail to grasp interrelation and proportion.

What are the prevailing impressions of evolution as viewed by different schools of thought? Beginning with materialistic science, it has made an effort to eliminate divinity from nature and man, or at least to crowd it back to the most remote protoplasmic energy. Secondary gods have been set up, and labelled "natural selection," "chemical affinity," "inherent energy," and "resident forces," in the attempt to make God unnecessary. It may be termed scientific polytheism; its homage is subtle, and is paid to secondary and dependent forces. But general unity, intelligence, and beneficence are not recognized. It is assumed that matter, through some mysterious inherent quality, virtually grows. In its conflict with theology, science has almost out-dogmatized the dogmatists by teaching a practical though unadmitted atheism.

The ranks of so-called orthodoxy are shaded, from those who still hold that a Deific fiat suddenly created all things from nothing, up to those who, in general, accept the evolutionary process of creation, especially in the lower grades of life. Even the liberals, however, find much difficulty in reconciling certain theological necessities — so supposed — with evolutionary facts in the domain of humanity. They are willing to indefinitely extend the creative period backward, and to concede the development theory as applied to organic life below man; but when he is reached, and the dogmas of original holiness, the "Fall," and the substitutionary atonement, are disturbed, there is but a faint or lame attempt at adjustment.

There is an impassable gulf between evolution and all special dispensations. If the established order has ever been abruptly broken into from without, upon any plane whatsoever, then evolution is a myth. God reigns in and through law, and is never self-contradictory.

There are other more consistent evolutionists, who logically avoid both of the extremes before noted. They see the Deity immanent in all his works, man included, moving in and through them towards a supreme and beautiful consummation.

The idolized forces of science are only differentiated forms of One Infinite Energy that is supremely intelligent and beneficent. Is it personal? Yes and no. How many swords have been crossed for lack of clear definitions! How vain to try to exactly fit weak, finite terms upon the Infinite! "Personal," to most minds, from its common associations, is unconsciously linked to changeableness, moods, states of mind, and limitations of locality, time, and space.

All *persons* make plans and change them. The Unchangeable — "the same yesterday, to-day, and forever" — makes no plans, and changes none. He is not less, but incomparably MORE, than personal. Infinite Mind, Love, and Law are terms which doubtless carry to the average mind a more correct concept of the Supreme Being than personality. But there is no objection to any term if it have no false association; for names are only labels, but ideas are vital. Finite judgment can only be made through attributes and manifestations.

This is not pantheism, neither does it remove God, or make him a mental abstraction. On the contrary, as we accustom ourselves to this larger idea, he becomes incomparably nearer and dearer. We then first really begin to feel the force of Paul's metaphysical declaration that "in Him we live and move and have our being." The traditional view is anthropomorphic, unscientific, and in reality irreligious. A natural reaction from such a narrow and irrational concept has logically produced many atheists and materialists.

When reverently followed, a true evolutionary philosophy leads up to the conclusion that all phenomena are the manifestations of one Infinite Mind. The Hebraic concept which pictured the Deity as a capricious force, who from the outside occasionally interfered with the cosmic economy, belongs to the evolutionary past. The divine methods are orderly,

Pantheism was blind, cold, and fatalistic, while spiritual unfoldment is a vital inspiration.

But although evolution as a process has been widely recognized, its supreme coronation is yet to take place. The materialism of Darwin still subtly lingers, and colors the researches and conclusions of the present leading evolutionary scientists. We are not disposed to criticise these eminent and able exponents of philosophical development; for they have all done a grand work for science, religion, and the world. But, with great deference, we shall try to show that the supreme recognition of applied evolution has not yet been generally made.

Darwinian evolution is deficient, in that it deals with forms and results rather than their immaterial causation. It is a progressive materialism. But it is indispensable as a stepping-stone to what is above it. Darwin and his co-laborers are entitled to the gratitude of the world for their great achievements and elaborations. Only through such untiring efforts could the lower steps and processes of the grand upward trend have been demonstrated.

Stripped of all technicality, and in the most concise general terms, the Darwinian philosophy may be stated substantially as follows: The first and lowest, or elemental plane contains inherent protoplasmic energy, diffused and unorganized, but potent in possibility. Here is resident vitality, but in a primal stage. The second grand plane is that of chemical compounds — a great step higher in quality, affinity, and determinateness; but organization is yet wanting. The next and third grand subdivision includes the vegetal kingdom. Energy has here been gathered, organized, classified, and individuated, as shown in a centred, manifested life. The fourth general plane of manifestation composes the kingdom of animal life. Locomotion, sensation, instinct, and will have been further added. Wonderful variety in comprehensive unity is displayed. Advancing another great step, humanity is reached, with its marvellous additional powers and capabilities. Reason, self-consciousness, and ethical discernment have come to the front, though they are still colored and swayed by a great residuum of passion, appetite, and self-seeking, which have come over from below.

Progress is always from the lower towards the higher, from the simple towards the more complex, and from the inorganic towards the organic, the latter by successive steps becoming higher and more intricate in organization. Each of the grand subdivisions, while possessing unmistakable unity and relation, shades almost imperceptibly into those adjoining it. The seeming exception to this is in the "missing link" between the animal and man. Progress is supposed to be through "natural selection" and the "survival of the fittest." Environment, and the consequent use and disuse of organs, together with sexual selection, are also important factors.

The weaker perish, while the stronger propagate their kind. Such is conventional evolution, stated in its briefest general terms.

But all this is only a moving succession of *visible forms*. It is everywhere assumed that these are the basic reality, while the life, mind, or soul manifested in them is only a property or function. If this be true, the immaterial part is clearly a dependent. Just here is the rank though subtle materialism which distinctly, though often unconsciously, permeates conventional science, philosophy, *materia medica*, and the organized church. By logical and fair inference from such a philosophy, man inherently belongs to the animal kingdom. But even in that kingdom he has no exclusive department of his own, being a vertebrate. In this more limited subdivision he still has no class of his own. He is simply a mammal. To be sure, he is a primate among mammals; but that distinction he also shares with the apes. His structural differences from them are comparatively slight. Thus man, if *he* be the *form*, is only an animal of a high order; or, more correctly, neither he nor the animal is more than a well-shaped mass of matter, having an attenuated dependent *property* called life or soul. But it could not be expected that Darwin would find everything. As a stepping-stone he was good in his order.

But though Spencer and others have greatly extended the Darwinian domain, refined it, and traced it upward, yet the essentially materialistic *basis* seems to be retained. Physical causation, or, in other words, life and mind, as the *result* rather than the *creator* of structural organism, is everywhere more or less distinctly assumed. While the high character of man as compared with his evolutionary brethren is admitted, he is yet regarded as a material, rather than an immaterial, entity. All would not insist that chemical changes in the brain are the cause of thoughts, or that that organ secretes consciousness and emotion as the liver secretes bile; yet, practically, such a philosophy, in various shades and degrees, is everywhere present.

Having thus briefly outlined "scientific" (materialistic) evolution, as at present accepted, let us sketch what we believe to be the truer and only logical view. It solves many problems, and dissipates numerous difficulties.

Evolution, in its essence and basis, is immaterial on the lower planes as well as the higher. The life, mind, or soul is always the cause and not the result of organization. In every case the unseen is the intrinsic entity. It follows that the real progression is in the ascending quality and complexity of mind, life, or soul, and not of matter. All of the advancing steps are successive states of internal character, and its visible form is only its outer resultant translation.

Matter, *per se*, never progresses. It is only an external, temporary banner or signboard. Identical physical material appears, disappears, and reappears in higher or lower shapes, as the case may be, and therefore can have no character of its own. It is clay grasped by the hand of a moulder. The elements which to-day make up the body of a dog or tree may have figured long ago in the material structure of a saint or philosopher. Assuredly there was no ascent or descent in the material, but only in its user. All the progress is in the unseen. The embodiment is not the progressive part, but just the well-fitting clothing which shows the quality and taste of its present owner. The human ego receives material into embodiment, and erects it into an animated form, and never makes a deviation in its shaping. If he drop the material, and it be utilized by a tiger life or mind, it at once assumes the corresponding feline expression in every detail. There is no exception to this rule. In the deepest analysis the *real tree* is the tree-life, and not the temporary material which it has laid hold of for outward expression. True, we may study and admire the latter, but it is unprofitable to mistake the picture for the substance.

Everything has a soul of some grade, and that includes all its present and future potentiality. Whether more or less advanced along the highway of individuation, all minds are, substantially, parts of the one divine, omnipresent Mind, which is the basis of all manifestation.

A piece of marble, or even a clod of earth, has a kind of life. Even were we to adopt the monistic theory, and infer that matter is solidified spirit, — perhaps its outermost and ultimate rim, — the order of expression remains unchanged.

It will be evident, then, that all true evolution is *metaphysical*. On the human plane it is also idealistic. This idealism is not of the Berkelian variety, which denies the existence of all objectivity, but of that practical quality which draws men forward. Upon all the subordinate planes progress seems to come from an unconscious pushing from behind, which is accompanied by friction. When the higher human department of spiritual intuition is reached, man begins intelligently to co-operate with law, and thereby gains its leverage. By learning to hold ideals before himself he powerfully contributes to his own unfoldment, and thus the "pushing" is supplemented. He divines how to "hitch his wagon to a star," and thus paves his onward path, and accelerates his progress God-ward.

> "From thee, great God, we spring, to thee we tend,
> Path, Motive, Guide, Original, and End."

In the great circle of creative development, the divine life and energy which God first *in*volved into the lowest conditions, is at length, through a series of grand steps, gathered, organized, individuated, and evolved into "sons of God," in which form, with reciprocal affection, the return is to be made to the "Father's House."

Let us now attempt the interpretation of what is known as the "Fall of Man," in the light of metaphysical evolution. A vital part of dogmatic theology is contained in the assumption that man was created pure and holy, and that through disobedience he fell. A substitutionary atonement was therefore legally necessary. The so-called "plan of salvation" is based upon the ruin which was caused by the single historic mistake. The remedial "scheme" consisted of a purchased release. Soften it as we may, it really amounts to a technical makeshift which God contrived after the defeat of his original plans. Practically the church is quietly slipping away from such a logic; but yet its authoritative doctrinal formulas remain unchanged. Though generally toned down in men's minds, it remains of life-size in the creeds. Salvation has been something done for and outside of one, on the condition of yielded assent to "the plan." It has been objective and historic, rather than subjective and present. A penalty has been *paid*, or rather, in effect, a link severed between cause and effect. This concept carries the inference that penalty is vindictive instead of corrective — antagonistic rather than reformatory.

Some of the visible branches of the great evolutionary tree seem to droop downward, and others entirely drop off, as externally observed. But all life and mind are conserved, however much outward forms may change or disintegrate. Occasional eddies or ebb-tides on the surface cannot invalidate the great universal upward trend.

How can the allegory of the "Fall" be naturally accounted for without any strained interpretation? Let us try to find a scientific, religious, and spiritual solution of this great tradition which will accord with reason and harmonize difficulties.

An allegory always has a meaning deeper than itself. The story of Adam and Eve portrays that period of transition when primeval man — the animal — evolved some moral character, and when reason measurably displaced instinct as the controlling force. The so-called first pair are types of the racial crossing of a great boundary line. Pre-Adamic man, being an animal, was not ashamed of his nakedness, and, in common with his kingdom, was governed by brutish instincts and appetites. He lived in dens and caves, and possessed only those faint foreshadowings of reason which we now behold in the highest animal intelligence.

But instinct, though low, is exact. In its wild native perfection it makes neither mistakes nor improvements. The bee of to-day, as of a thousand years ago, always forms the honey-cell in perfect geometrical proportion; and the web of the spider was ever, as now, a marvel of regularity and proportion. The bird makes no mistake in singing its song, or in building its nest; and the beaver even adapts his dam in advance to the clemency or inclemency of the coming season. The all-pervading divine life and wisdom resident in the animal shines through, reflecting its uniformity and perfection, though in actual expression it cannot rise higher than its low plane and crude medium.

Bearing in mind the definition of instinct, we pass to note that Eden does not represent spiritual, or even intellectual, satisfaction, but only that which is sensuous. Primeval man at length reached the climax of his physical development. To his consciousness there was nothing higher. Every known want was satisfied. There was neither moral nor spiritual law to be observed or violated. He had no unsatisfied longing or aspiration. A great evolutionary epoch was completed, and the cup of sensory enjoyment was full. There were no mistakes to be rectified, and no sins to bring disquietude. THAT WAS EDEN. It represents the ripeness and perfection of a great kingdom.

But at length the God-voice in man became audible, and the throes and birth-pangs of a new kingdom began. Reason — now infantile and tottering — came upon the stage, and stumblings and mistakes became the rule. The gestatory period of the higher selfhood had passed, and the moral freedom of choice and of possible voluntary character came to light.

Man forever lost his sense of completeness in animal development, and a rational and spiritual restlessness possessed him. There was no more Eden. The "flaming sword which turned every way" was the evolutionary bar which unceasingly interdicted a return to perfect sensuous repose and satisfaction. The rational and moral nature passed from latency to activity. Gestation was ended, the umbilic cord severed, and man was cast out, to begin at the very foundation to build a new consciousness, and project a higher kingdom.

The mistakes connected with infantile and ignorant choosing are typified by thorns and thistles, toil and sweat. The perfect delight of Eden was missing. This, to the childish stage of human consciousness, seemed like a great loss — a "fall." What a natural and reasonable basis for the great tradition!

Although the story of Adam and Eve apparently refers to a brief episode, the actual transition covers an evolutionary epoch not yet completed. Eden has gone beyond repair; but the succeeding kingdom, even at the present time, is only in its childish stage.

The "Fall," though from perfect material satisfaction to a constant divine restlessness, is *upward*. The attainments of voluntary moral and spiritual character are only possible within the limits of their own kingdom, and must begin with the stumblings, educational mistakes (sins), and discipline of an experience outside of Eden. A child does not learn to walk without a few falls, but as soon as he understands the law of walking he need not continue falling. Eden means ignorance as well as innocence. Man must partake of the fruit of the tree of the "knowledge of good and evil," in order to discover the beauty and goodness of the good, and the value of its cultivation. Character, like thorns and thistles, only grows beyond the boundaries of Edenic beguilement. There must be a free choice of good from the midst of the abundance of its opposite; for even virtue involuntarily imposed is slavish and stale.

But the thorns and thistles beyond Eden are transformable by the "fallen" or rather the new man into blooming and fruitful bowers. Having developed the power to re-form, he becomes — by virtue of the divinity within him — a secondary creator. The thorns and thistles are found to be not "evil," but only unripened and undeveloped good. Edenic products come spontaneously; but after falling upward, man — real man — forms for himself. He has become as "a god," but even down to the close of the nineteenth century is still largely unconscious of it. Potentially he can take of the endless abundance of unmanifest good, and organize and express the same.

It is by the higher development of the intuitional and spiritual faculties — the divinity within — that man comes into conformity to the established order, blesses the ground that was "cursed," and is introduced into a new paradise infinitely superior to the old Eden. The toil and sweat now need come only in an effort to go backward. They are the "flaming sword," which, however, is more kindly to men than they are to themselves, because it forever bars them out of the captivating though deadly anæsthesia of the Edenic paradise. The "Fall of Man" was a leap upward and onward. It was not only necessary, but good. Only by some experimental infraction of the higher law could its principles be discovered, and at length fully interpreted. But, having learned it, man need not longer "kick against the pricks" in order to find that they are sharp.

Things are lower or higher in their progressive relation, but there is no "evil" as an objective force or principle. The condition, so termed, is an inversion or attempted going back. Any plane viewed from the altitude of a higher one seems evil from relativity, rather than opposing abstract quality. Evolution is a ladder with many rounds. The lower ones, as steps, are useful in their times and places, but if lingered upon, a growth of thorns twines about them to urge us onward. The vital energy which men thoughtlessly squander, when turned higher is of supreme value as a motor. The animal in man — and every man has one — is not an enemy to be extirpated, but an able-bodied servant to be trained, controlled, and made an efficient helper.

In the human domain, evolution starts with the Adam, and has the Christ for its ideal and ultimate climax. The transition must be subjectively actualized in every human being. Adam is the concept of self as a physical body. Christ is the *knowledge* of self as mind, soul, spirit — divinity within. To wait for the evolution of the spiritual consciousness until after the event called death is to squander the divine birthright and heritage.

The supreme feature in the brilliant after-glow of the nineteenth century is the discovery that man does not need to wait to be pushed from behind, and torn by evolutionary friction, but that he can voluntarily unfold himself and escape it. Displacing a material with the spiritual consciousness lawfully assures progress. It is practically the "Christ-mind" in humanity, or the general incarnation. The single historic ideal was a first fruit, or really a life-size picture of man. The present universal spiritual gestation will end in a new evolutionary nativity.

The great upward trend, with its all-inclusive scope, brushes away all pessimism, and its numerous brood of uncanny shadows and spectres. When rightly interpreted, these and all other human woes are but temporary wayside prods, to hurry us along to higher and more beautiful outlooks. To turn back is to invite friction. To drop down in conditions is to make them more binding; but partnership with law recreates them. We must focus our vision upon the expanding divinity within, which has long ago been involved, and is now pressing for expressive evolvement.

OMNIPRESENT DIVINITY.

THIS is a scientific age. The domain of exact investigation is visibly broadening, and limitations are being pushed back in all directions. There have been other periods noted for their intellectual activity in certain directions, during which lofty climaxes have been reached. Great waves of architectural and artistic accomplishment, and eras of scholastic research in philosophy, theology, ethics, and jurisprudence, have risen to flood-tide, and finally receded to make room for their respective incoming successors. The manuscripts and tomes of the world have been crowded with facts and truths, and these have been heaped up in unrelated piles until their apexes reached as high as the breadth of their respective bases would permit. The artist, philosopher, geologist, astronomer, theologian, physician, scientist, economist, and jurist, each independent of the others, staked out his own territory, surveyed its boundaries, erected a high fence around it, and then proceeded to build thereupon. Imposing intellectual pyramids have thus been reared with painstaking accuracy, but each has been distinct and unrelated. Like a gigantic mathematical puzzle, all these departments have been in irregular-shaped fragments, and no one could fit them together. Facts, when isolated, are not facts, and truths out of relation tell lies.

In the present paper, the fourth and final of this series[1] upon the great kingdom of mind and its relations, it seems logical to conclude with a synthetic though concise survey. A study of the parts from the standpoint of the whole is as interesting and profitable as is the converse, and far less common. It is true that some advanced theologians have given us very attractive concepts and glimpses of the "Immanent God;" but much remains to be done to bring this stupendous truth into the narrow, crowded, materialistic consciousness.

While specialty of pursuit is an obvious present characteristic, a deeper survey reveals a remarkable levelling of barriers and a general unification. The world has been crowded with acquired knowledge, so called, nine-tenths of which has been not only useless but misleading. To have a great stock of facts at command was to be "learned." Education consists in packing them in tiers in the human mind. Even if they were rubbish they made an imposing appearance. The man who had the most showy mental storehouse, with its shelves all labelled, towered above his fellows.

---

[1] Originally used in connection with, and related to, the **three** preceding.

But a great change is apparent. The features in high relief at the close of the nineteenth century are interrelation and reinterpretation. A thousand disjointed truths are found to be meaningless; for it is only *truths in relation* that lead to *the Truth*. Only when dovetailed together do they acquire value. As Pope aptly observes: —

> "Not chaos-like together crush'd and bruis'd,
> But as the world, harmoniously confus'd,
> Where order in variety we see,
> And where, though all things differ, all agree."

The synthetic method constitutes the present renaissance. The leading factors that are involved in the ushering in of the new dispensation are the evolutionary philosophy, the recognition of law as universal, and the third and greatest, — only yet in its dawn in the human consciousness, — the discovery that the established order is beneficent, and that only.

> "O happiness! our being's end and aim!
> Good, pleasure, ease, content! whate'er thy name:
> That something still which prompts the eternal sigh,
> For which we bear to live, or dare to die."

The kingdom of heaven is at length philosophically interpreted as a subjective condition rather than an objective locality. Nineteen centuries ago the Christ-quality which found early and complete expression through the personality of Jesus distinctly declared that it "is within you," but until now the world has hardly been evolved up to the level of such a comprehension. As the law of the spiritual domain is discerned, the subjective elements which constitute that "kingdom" — which though immaterial may be present here and now — are scientifically recognized. The spiritual chemism which selects and intelligently combines the necessary constituents for this grand consummation in man is as exact and orderly as is the material compounding of the laboratory.

Either section of a beautiful polished sphere that has been shattered in twain is no more incomplete and fragmentary than is a science which is unspiritual, or a religion that is unscientific. Each when severed from its counterpart is not only arbitrary and abnormal, but misleading. The outcome in one case is a capricious supernaturalism, and in the other, a pessimistic materialism. Either one, untempered by its complement, is false. Congruity, adaptability, and beauty are set at naught, law dishonored, and the cosmos made to appear chaotic. To constructively bring together in the human mind these apparently ragged fragments in their true unity is the grandest work of this remarkable epoch.

Evolution, for so long regarded as atheistic and irreligious, and even yet tolerated by many only because of its cumulative and irresistible proofs, has done more to build up an intelligent consciousness of the One Infinite Intelligence, Goodness, and Will, than all the dogmatic formulas extant.

Descartes took a few detached facts, and studied them in relation. Darwin fitted in many more. Wallace increased the stock, and Spencer made immense additions on every side. The Great Unit has now grown, so that it is certain that niches will be found for all the fragmentary facts of the past.

But the greatest intuitive mind of modern times, who instinctively *saw* and *felt* the oneness and interrelation of all things, was Emerson. He was the fittest channel through which the combined ripened inspiration of the past could become focalized and articulated in the present era. The materialistic evolutionists wrought upon the outer crust among details, while his spiritual perception penetrated through and through. He refined and translated mechanical sequences, and pierced their outer coverings to the divinity within. He also divined that the one great human complement is conformity to law. That genial and spiritual philosopher, Henry Drummond, has also done noble service in the release of the minds of men from a supposed capriciousness of executive will in the spiritual realm.

Omnipresent Divinity, or the Allness of the Good, though taught by the highest and truest interpretation of the Christian Scriptures, and also in sacred writings other than the Hebraic, has been too transcendent a truth to find easy lodgment in the unspiritual, or even in the intellectual understanding. The ancient seers, who in varying degree were spiritual experts, had visions and experiences of it, and it had temporary manifestation in the days of the primitive church. But notably in the time of Constantine, when church and state became allied, there was a decline from spiritual purity and power to an intellectual and scholastic dogmatism, characterized by a great influx of creeds, ceremonies, apologetics, and controversies. The anthropomorphous idea of God was absorbed from the heathen nations, and even yet it is not displaced. A deific " Person" who will change his plans upon importunity, susceptible to improvement upon human suggestion, having various limitations, and working the universe from the outside, has been the mental concept of the Eternal Spirit in the average human consciousness. While with their lips and theories men have spoken of Infinite, Omniscient, Omnipresent Love, Will, and Intelligence, they have held in their thoughts an image, limited, local, and personal, often substantially a telescopic likeness of themselves.

A philosophical and vital at-one-ment with the divine mind and method should supersede the technical, commercial, supernatural, and super-reasonable atonement. No artificial objective bargain or purchase through physical blood and suffering can sever cause and effect, or formally restore violated order. Such a belief has made men careless of conformity to divine law, because they counted upon the possession of this magic subterfuge.

To misinterpret the supreme love and goodness of the Divine Mind deranges the beautiful and normal relation between Divinity and humanity. The established order has never been abruptly broken into, and never will be. It is transcendently grand, beautiful, and harmonious. Human wisdom and importunity cannot improve it, for it needs no revision. Only conformity therewith, in thought, understanding, and consciousness, can fill the cup of human satisfaction and felicity. Such a supernal philosophy when thoroughly assimilated will, from its very nature, heal human ills on every plane of expression. Man's idea of God is the very corner-stone, not only of his wholeness and happiness, but of his very being.

The dogmatic concept of the Holy Spirit as an infrequent supernatural influence "sent" or "poured out" by degrees, in response to importunity, literally means that Omnipresent Divinity is extremely variable in its omnipresence. Man has thus tried to fasten upon God the changeable states of his own consciousness.

> "But greatness which is infinite makes room
> For all things in its lap to lie;
> We should be crushed by a magnificence
> Short of infinity."

The scientific (exact, true, and lawful) Holy Spirit

is an ever-present, practical, every-day force, which will occupy the soul-consciousness of man as he gives it room. It is a "Present Help," or only another name for Omnipresent Good.

Can it be said that such a divine philosophy in any way dishonors or undermines religion (from *religere*, to bind to God) when compared with the past supernaturalism? Just the reverse. It not only honors and confirms everything that is pure and good in religion, — as a life, — but it consecrates all the other departments of human activity, and lifts them to a supernal level. It makes *all* truth religious truth, and *all* life divine life. It purifies the whole discordant realm of the "common and unclean" which has so long darkened and benumbed human consciousness.

The fish in the sea might as reasonably bewail the absence of water as for man to theorize about the "withdrawal" of the Spirit. Perhaps the denizens of the deep could not become oblivious to the surrounding medium; but it *is* quite possible for man, owing to the free moral choice of the ego, to shut even the Universal Entity out of his consciousness. Although immersed in it, yet, measurably, *to him* it is not only far away, but really non-existent. It was formerly said that it had been "grieved away," or had "taken its flight," which means that man had only closed his eyes, or rather his thoughts. The vital importance of the cultivation of the creative thinking-faculty, set forth in a former paper, will be especially manifest in this connection.

Paul's immortal aphorism, "In him we live and move and have our being," is no less scientific than religious. The resurrection of modern science will take place when it bestows some attention upon mind as well as matter, thoughts as well as molecules, soul as well as body, the spiritual as well as the material; and when it recognizes that *law* is as imperiously exact upon the immaterial plane as upon that of sense. Material science is not to be ignored or left uncultivated, but supplemented, rounded out, and interpreted. But when severed from its relations, even its axioms are untruthful.

The limitations of God that have dwelt in the minds of men have been the basis of prevailing limitations in human expression. The kind of a deity that one worships, whether formally or informally, at once determines the status of the worshipper. Idolatry, though unconscious, is perhaps as general in Christendom as elsewhere. Among the so-called "heathen," at least with all the more intelligent classes, the "graven image" is only a symbol, or a visible fulcrum to aid in mental concentration. Unseen graven images are a thousand-fold more numerous than the visible idols of heathendom. Not only do men "fall down" before the blandishments of wealth, luxury, passion, power, and sensuous pursuit, but they substitute a great variety of blind forces for the One Force, and of unrealities for the ideal Reality.

As the Absolute, Unlimited, and Unconditioned are incomprehensible to the human mind, the highest subjective ideal of which the individual is capable receives the adoration. By immutable law man grows into the likeness and conforms to the quality of his Model. All growth is through ideals, but among them all each man always has *one* which to him is supreme.

The divine nativity being universal, man is ever restless until he returns to the "Father's House," and finds the counterpart and complement of his being. Deeply imbedded in his very constitution, there is a subtle soul-hunger which — as demand always presupposes supply — will at length be satisfied. Pursuit in the wrong direction, and ignorant, unsuccessful searches for the normal divine satisfaction, make up those appearances which we call evil, disorder, disease, fear, grief, sin, and pessimism. All these negatives and deficiencies are not entities, but distorted and fragmentary views, delusive and mistaken impressions of the great Ideal. The whole objective cosmos is orderly and good, but the clouded and warped subjective lens colors the universe to the observer. The soul-vibrations are discordant with the chords and tones of the divine economy.

Man is immersed in an infinitude of unmanifested Good (God), and it presses in upon him in order that he may embody and express it. Vibration with its harmonies makes him transparent in soul, so that it shines through him without obstruction. Materialism clouds and thickens such clearness into opacity, and friction is the result.

The bewildered mentality evolves its own spectres, and clothes and arms them with fantastic terrors; and they people the thought domain, and, in due time, press forward for ultimate or physical expression. These dark shadows — for they have no positive reality — have all been named, crowned, and subjectively materialized, until they have become a great host of leering demons. For ages we have been descending to their own plane, and there waging an unsuccessful and perpetual warfare against them. We have vainly expected to conquer demons with demons, evils with evils, and shadows with shadows. We have fought with rusty and untempered material weapons, but have left in its scabbard the keen and glittering " sword of the Spirit."

Among the latest therapeutic refinements, we essay to drive out diseases with their own kind and relation slightly toned down through "cultures." We even poison the blood of our innocent and unsuspecting equine servitors, and then transfuse this abnormal sanguinary abomination (anti-toxine) into our own economy, expecting to cast out evil with evil. It has also been reserved for this highly developed age to torture animal sensibility — in the name of science — with wholesale vivisection, in order to study prolonged agony. We may well exclaim with Madame Roland (slightly paraphrased), "O Science! Science! how many crimes are committed in thy name!" Cultures of disease-germs are made, multiplied, and sent out in the interest of so-called science. Evil will never be exterminated by sowing its seeds broadcast, even though they be somewhat diluted in quality. Only light can dispel darkness, and only good can drive out its opposite. "God made man upright" (ideally and potentially), "but they have sought out many inventions."

To open the recesses of the soul to the ever-present Universal Goodness is to displace all distorted negatives. They cannot abide the divine companionship. Conscious communion and oneness with exuberant, all-abounding Life and Wholeness sweep out all beliefs of the power of evil; for there is but one real objective Power in the universe, and that is Good. If there were other and adverse forces, Good could not be omnipresent and unlimited.

The Rev. A. W. Jackson, in his splendid little work, "The Immanent God," recalls the impressions of his early childhood regarding the Deity. They are so typical and widely representative that they are of instructive interest. Recounting them, he says: "Over my head, in the first place, was a firm-set Mosaic firmament. Reared on this was a vast oval throne, around which were troops of angels, ever in readiness to praise or serve. Beside this throne, on a lower seat, sat the Christ, with benignity and mercy in his look; and on the throne itself a figure of a man of vast size, with round cheeks covered with beard, sitting in imperturbable majesty, surveying the world and issuing decrees respecting it, and looking down with calm severity upon the deeds of men."

This may appear childish, yet such a mental picture, refined and expanded in varying degree, has formed the basis of much of the theology of the past. In a crude way it delineates that which has been inferred from dogma, gathered from hymnology, out-pictured by poetry, and interpreted from the superficial *letter* of Scripture, and by these means firmly lodged in the human mind. Even yet the hard outlines of such materialistic idolatry are but slowly dissolving. In a peculiar sense it is subjectively true that each worshipper creates — in and for himself — his own deity. He pays homage to his individual concept of the Reality rather than to the Reality itself.

It is clearly obvious that an ideal which may be defined as Omnipresent Love, Law, Life, Spirit, and Goodness is higher, purer, and more ennobling than one which would naturally be conveyed by the term "Person." This is yet further evident when the word takes on additional limitation from its usual representative pronoun " He." This comment is only made to call attention to the bald poverty of conventional language. We take cheap terms with commonplace associations, and from force of habit stamp them upon the Infinite. The terms employed should be vehicles for the highest ideals, and, so far as is possible, unweighted by limitations.

But even in sacred literature we find deific appellations which are not only limited, but, by association, unmoral, if not immoral. A few of these are Lord, King, Sovereign, Ruler, Judge, and Potentate. The associations connected with the general personal use of these terms have been largely autocratic, despotic, oppressive, vain, and sensuous. They have humanized God, and not spiritualized man. Oriental monarchs and despots left their stamp upon these official titles long before there was any general idea of human brotherhood and unity. Bearing in mind the wonderful moulding power of thought, what a contrast between the past concept of the "dread Sovereign of the skies" and the supreme consciousness of the Universal Life and our oneness with it! The latter ideal, held in the field of mental vision, sends an influx of vital invigoration even down to the subsoil of the physical organism.

When man turns his gaze God-ward, that which he sees is colored by subjective states and prejudices. Jealousy, wrath, and anger have been looked upon as divine features; and the crude pictures of the

Deity that have crowded the human mind have
represented him as cruel, as mocking at calamity,
fond of flattery, and with innumerable other human
foibles and prejudices. Under the discordant and
depressing mental idolatries of the past, it is not
strange that such a general nightmare has brought
into manifestation a great host of mental and physical inharmonies and disorders. The idea, or the
ideal, of God shapes the deep formative basis of
human expression. A distorted view of the "All in
All" produces a universal eclipse of Goodness, and
renders normality and sanity almost impossible.

In the light of the great truth that universal law
is beneficent, adversity disappears, discord is transformed, evil dissolves, the Sun of righteousness
(right thinking) arises, illness is healed, and darkness flees away. We are backed by the forces of the
universe if we adopt its methods and vibrate with
its harmonies. The host of subjective spectres, demons, and torments are only bats and shadows which
disappear into nothingness when the white light of
Omnipresent Divinity floods the consciousness. This
is not poetic imagery, but belongs to the new scientific recognition of the higher thought. To "practise
the presence of God" is no strange, illogical exercise, but a rational, every-day accomplishment.

Everything is secular, and everything divine, and
all life is included in the One Life. Heaven is
neither more nor less than conformity to law upon

every plane. It involves a displacement of all negatives and deficiencies with an overshadowing consciousness of the All-Good. In proportion as divinity at the soul-centre is recognized and held as normal, the visible circumference, with all its dependent relations, will fall into line. In the profoundest sense there is but One Mind and Life, and all individuated expressions of this Universal become dry and barren when out of conscious connection with their great Primal Fountain. With open conduits ever maintained, the supply is perennial and overflowing.

MENTAL AND PHYSICAL CHEMISTRY IN THE HUMAN ECONOMY.

THE human body is a chemical laboratory. The mind is the conscious or unconscious chemist, and exercises direct control in all the multiform physical processes. Its compounding is performed unintelligently, and often ignorantly, but the final product is always the natural outcome of past and present mental activity, in quality and degree. The subtle delicacy and complexity of the chemical transmutations which are ever succeeding each other in the physical organism are unparalleled in the most exhaustive experiments of the best-equipped external laboratories. The possible knowledge of the trained technical expert is but rudimentary in comparison with the marvellous skill of the invisible thought chemist, whose work, though carried on sub-consciously or in secret, is at length known and read of all men.

The growing interest in psychological research, or soul-study, especially in its relation to the body, is manifested not only in a general curiosity about phenomena as such, but in a laudable search for the underlying truth, and especially that which is practical and useful. There is, however, too much of a desire for what is merely strange and marvellous. In this practical age, whenever new theories are proposed, the first question should be, How much truth do they contain? and, second, How can this truth be best applied for the benefit of humanity? Does the thing offered promise, in any measure, to lessen prevailing infelicity, and to promote the welfare and upliftment of mankind?

The general interest in the dynamics of mind is also evident from the attention which is being bestowed upon the subject in colleges and universities. Psychology has now a well-established place in the curriculum of all the larger educational institutions. Several of these contain psycho-physical laboratories carefully equipped for experiment and research.

But it is uniformly the case that when any new truth is recognized, some old doctrines that have been accepted for truth must be displaced, or else given a new interpretation. The spirit of conventionalism tends to make existing institutions extremely conservative, and often rather intolerant of new advances in human thought. That which *is*, is usually self-sufficient, so that new truth meets with some friction before finding its thorough assimilation. This is seen in the tardy recognition given by established systems to the practical possibilities of mental and spiritual science. Every great advance in its early aspects has seemed like a strange, and often unwelcome, intruder. But all truth which the world needs will be restless, and even aggressive, until it glides into its rightful place and finds application.

Within the broadened scope of scientific research which has recently been instituted by the government at Washington for the increase of knowledge through study and experiment, is one department which is called psycho-physics. A very complete laboratory has been organized in the Smithsonian Institute under the direction of Professor Elmer Gates (now of Philadelphia), an eminent scientist who for many years has been pursuing a series of unique studies which are very suggestive. He is not a psychologist or metaphysician, so that all his investigations have been from the materialistic standpoint of a physicist. But owing to his originality, thoroughness, and the peculiar line of his studies, the conclusions that he has reached are of remarkable import to the scientific world. His specialty is described as "the newest of the sciences," and he deals with matters which hitherto have been regarded as beyond the field of exact investigation. The great interest which attaches to his discoveries is found in the fact that physics, when thoroughly interpreted, necessarily leads to the indorsement of metaphysics; or, in other words, the claims of mental science as to the power of thought for the upbuilding or pulling down of the bodily energies are positively confirmed by chemical tests and measurements.

The fact has been demonstrated that there is a supremely important realm of psycho-physical law and truth that has been left unrecognized and unutilized, but which has recently been coming into distinct outline in the human understanding. It may be compared to an unexplored territory towards which adventurous explorers are approaching on different sides; or to a lofty mountain peak, towards which, by different routes and unseen by each other, various climbers are toiling up, to gain the broad outlook and secure a vantage ground from which there may be a clear view into a hitherto strange and undiscovered country.

This novel and unfamiliar realm is made up of the broad truth of mental causation and the formative power of thought as expressed in the physical chemistry of the human organism. The existence of this energy, the laws through which it operates, their utilization, wonderful adaptibility and potency, all together make up the strange country — till recently the *terra incognita* of human attainment.

But looking upon another side, we find that a small but earnest band of noble souls, undeterred by the fear of unpopularity, undismayed by flippant criticism and scholastic satire, and impelled by a spiritual intuition which is an enigma to the world at large, had already scaled these heights of "Pisgah," and gained a clear view of the promised land. Guided by a keen inner perception, this brave and scattered minority, whose names are not enrolled upon the annals of science, reached the goal of high principle, and from their lofty vantage ground proclaim liberty to all the people.

They have interpreted and made known "the mystery of the ages," and brought into the light of noonday that ideal *summum bonum* of which the past has afforded only dim and uncertain glimpses. Its partial and occasional outcroppings as recorded in history, which have vaguely been regarded as capricious, supernatural, and super-reasonable, are being retranslated, and a misunderstood mass of chaotic phenomena brought into harmonious regularity.

But, as already indicated, the important development of the present time is that the advance pickets of physical science are coming up to the summit of truth, on another side and by a different route. Through the slower processes of intellectual logic and chemical demonstration, they have toiled up until their extreme advance is almost face to face with the metaphysical minority which for some time has occupied the ground. The supposed "weak things" of the world confounded the strong; for the quiet, silent climbers scaled these heights well in advance. The rigid forms of institutionalism are slow and clumsy in their adaptive conformity to human needs, for they only move forward with great friction.

But let us note more specifically the latest developments in this so-called newest department of science. The recently heralded discoveries tentatively approach a position already familiar to the few who first arrived by the lighter and easier intuitional path. These were able to penetrate the mists of materialism, and to perceive the desired goal and make directly for it. They, however, most cordially welcome their brethren who are arriving by the route of sensuous measurement. We give them hearty greetings; and now let us note their first impressions of this higher realm in their own language. It will be necessary to give quotations at some length, in order to convey their full import.

In a very carefully recorded statement recently made, Professor Gates gives some of the conclusions arrived at from his exhaustive and long-continued experiments. He says:—

"I have discovered that bad and unpleasant feelings create harmful chemical products in the body, which are physically injurious. Good, pleasant, benevolent, and cheerful feelings create beneficial chemical products which are physically healthful. These products may be detected by chemical analysis in the perspiration and secretions of the individual. I have detected more than forty of the bad, and as many of the good."

"Suppose half a dozen men in a room. One feels depressed, another remorseful, another ill-tempered, another jealous, another cheerful, and another benevolent. It is a warm day; they perspire. Samples of their perspiration are placed in the hands of the psycho-physicist. Under his examination they reveal all those emotional conditions distinctly and unmistakably."

CHEMISTRY IN THE HUMAN ECONOMY. 219

"To sum it up, it is found that for each bad emotion there is a corresponding chemical change in the tissues of the body which is life-depressing and poisonous. Contrariwise, every good emotion makes a life-promoting change. A noble and generous action blesses the doer as well as the beneficiary. Every thought which enters the mind is registered in the brain by a change in the structure of its cells. The change is a physical change, more or less permanent."

"Anybody may go into the business of building his own mind. The thinking organ undergoes perpetual changes in cell-structure, and is never finished."

"Even in old age it is not too late. Let the esoteric mind-builder systematically devote an hour each day to calling up pleasant ideas and memories. Let him summon those finer feelings of benevolence and unselfishness which are called up in ordinary life only now and then. Let him make this a regular exercise, like swinging dumbbells. Let him gradually increase the time devoted to these psychical gymnastics, giving them sixty or ninety minutes per diem."

"At the end of a month he will find the change in himself surprising. The alteration will be apparent in his actions and thoughts. It will have been registered in the cell-structure of his brain. Cells useful for good thinking will have been well developed, while others productive of evil will have shrunk. Morally speaking, the man will be a great improvement on his former self. Such training is most profitably conducted under the instruction of a skilled psycho-physicist. One result will be to increase and quicken the power of original thinking. In other words, inventors can be made to order, and discovery can be promoted. Genius has been an accident hitherto; in the future it will be created systematically."

We have made the above quotations quite at length, to show somewhat in detail the latest conclusions of physical science as given by one of its most eminent exponents. It is interesting to note how strongly the trend is in the line of metaphysical thought and spiritual evolution. Professor Gates has no avowed sympathy with mental healing, as such; but in his recorded investigations as a physicist he has virtually demonstrated, through chemical analysis, its most fundamental claims. The sprinkling of unconventional souls who have been struggling to bring these great truths into general recognition have known them all along; but now science has actually demonstrated them by its own methods. They are found to have a positive chemical basis and proof.

It is therefore the deliberate and latest conclusion of institutional science, that for each morbid or unwholesome mental state there is a corresponding degeneration in the bodily tissues. The more intense the conditions, the more poisonous and life-depressing the natural product which logically follows. Contrariwise, every noble, pure, and lofty emotion actually adds to the life-promoting forces. Science has therefore come to the conclusion that it pays to think high, even for one's own physical welfare.

As stated in the quotations, different qualities of thought, besides weaving their quality into the whole physical organism, gradually index themselves in appropriate brain-cells. High moral or spiritual thinking sets the blood to coursing towards the crown of the head. An activity is induced, which perceptibly raises the temperature of that section of the brain, so that it may be easily measured externally.

CHEMISTRY IN THE HUMAN ECONOMY. 221

When such activity habitually continues, new brain-cells are formed and invigorated. The same rule holds good with other faculties which have their correspondences in different parts of the brain. The skull is therefore the outward index of the qualitative energy which the *man* is exercising inside.

Materialistic science from the very method of its researches has usually been color blind to mental and spiritual entities. It deals with matter, and with forces supposedly blind and unreasoning, and works only from a physical standpoint and hypothesis. Its measures, tests, and weights are applied to results rather than causes. Its diagnosis does not go deeper than symptoms. Even when admitting that thought has a kind of force, the opinion is still held among high authorities that mind is really automatic. Man is interpreted as a physical instrument acted upon and swayed by sentient forces, rather than a divine soul or ego whose high vocation should be to grasp these energies and rule and wield them.

But signs of advancement multiply. The daily psycho-physical exercises recommended by Professor Gates are really mental healing and spiritual culture and unfoldment under a more high-sounding and scientific label. It is most encouraging to realize that the statements of so eminent and thorough a scientist will carry conviction in many quarters where metaphysical testimony to the same effect would be lightly regarded. But Professor Gates is far in advance of institutional teaching and textbooks in general, and the logical deductions from his experiments will but gradually find acceptance in scientific circles. The idea of a necessary physical basis and causation for all phenomena is so strongly rooted in the minds of men that facts are misinterpreted, spiritual vision blurred, and human emancipation from the lower nature postponed. Professional deductions are generally limited to such facts as can be tested by measurement, temperature, and physical energy. But inner consciousness and soul-development elude even the most searching tests of the laboratory. From the low standpoint of physics nothing beyond its own realm can be discerned.

But it may be of interest to take some of the weighed and measured facts as shown by psycho-physical research, and subject them to a higher and truer interpretation. For instance, we are aware that the human stomach is the most important chemical agency in the physical economy of man. When the digestive processes are badly performed, and a lack of assimilative energy causes a deterioration of the blood, the organ is generally subjected to medication, with the hope that through such treatment it will regain its normal efficiency. The mental state is not taken into account. But a deeper study shows that the mind is the governor. The digestive energy of the same stomach, with the same kind of nourishment, depends upon the mental state. If

CHEMISTRY IN THE HUMAN ECONOMY.

the important nerves which centre in this leading organ are disturbed by anger, fear, grief, jealousy, or any other serious discord, there is a general suspension of functional activity. The difficulty, under usual conditions, is not with the food, nor with the stomach, nor even with the nerves, but with what is back of and above all these secondary agencies. The chemical condition of the human body, in quality and detail, is a mirror-like reflection of its mental chemistry in the past.

Says Amelia Barr, in one of her interesting tales : " For who takes cold or receives injury while the spirit has the upper hand ? Men and women, driven by great enthusiasms, go through fire and water, and compass impossibilities. All our limitations are of the body; but in our diviner moments, when the soul takes command, it makes but small account of them."

Out of his rich spiritual perception Henry Ward Beecher said : " So out of that state of mind which was implied when Christ wrought healing, came the spiritual power that took on a physical result. We do not yet know what the hidden power of the soul is. There are all around the world, breaking out in irregular ways, instances of the power of certain states of mind."

We are well aware that the laws of chemistry are absolutely exact, and always the same. To form a given product, the necessary proportion of the various ingredients must be known and carefully conformed to in every successful experiment. The chemist takes a just pride in the delicate accuracy of all his tests and measurements. He uses the most sensitive instruments, observing carefully every possible condition that may have the slightest bearing upon the result.

But in the higher chemistry of thought and spirit how little of such painstaking accuracy has been observed! But the law of chemical combination in mind is as exact and unvarying as in physics or the arts, and of what incomparable importance! The druggist filters and purifies his ingredients, and blends them with the utmost care, in order to produce a perfect compound. Sometimes a very slight variation in the proportion of substances will result in crystalline forms of the most diverse order.

There is good reason to believe that early in the twentieth century there will be truly scientific remedial formulas generally utilized from the chemistry of a higher and diviner realm. Psychological chemism embraces the deeper education of thought, and the scientific building of character. How crudely this work is conventionally carried on! What an attempted blending of insoluble elements, and what an unscientific method, with the vain hope of an ideal result!

Into the sensitive and responsive recesses of the child-mind is poured a mass of conglomerate material, well mixed with repression, limitation, and negation; and the result is termed "education." Little is educed, but much is learned that were better unlearned. A soul-structure to be symmetrical must be carefully and intelligently compounded. If the intellectual elements are destitute of any conserving and purifying mixture of intuitive and spiritual ingredients, the combination lacks vital power and proportion. The ego must select pure and wholesome materials, and blend them in normal and harmonious proportion. *True education consists in training the thought to train itself.* The imaging faculty, like the tongue, is an unruly member until it is tamed and brought into subjection, but rightly governed it becomes a most efficient instrument and restorative. The negative elements of selfishness, animalism, avarice, and envy in human character, will continually produce mould, acidity, fermentation, scum, and dregs, unless the rectifying agency of love be added, to blend and sweeten the otherwise refractory mixture. We must have the nourishment of vital spiritual dynamics rather than an infantile dependence upon externals.

Man cannot live by bread alone. We must unlearn much worldly wisdom, to make room for the higher education. Our curriculum must be as broad as humanity, and as high as divinity; but we must cultivate a child-like transparency and simplicity. By earnestly turning our gaze inward, we discover that the mind of man is the grandest force in existence, and that truth is its great complement. We must bore artesian wells through the stratified crust of human thought, from which shall spout up pure and life-giving water, which will quench the soul-thirst of humanity. We must discover the divine image and life within the soul, and give the *logos* articulate expression. Our brothers and sisters must be taken by the hand, and led up into the "Mount of Transfiguration," and Law and Prophecy be retranslated until they appear in the human consciousness clothed in garments white and glistering. Divine incarnations must be multiplied and perfected, until God shall find adequate expression in humanity.

The Rosicrucians made a careful search for a life-giving specific, and faithfully tried to heal human ills. But their search was not successful. Ponce de Leon thought he had discovered the fountain of perpetual youth in Florida, and very recently a modern scientist announced the finding of the veritable "elixir of life." But notwithstanding all these repeated disappointments, there is a true *elixir vita*. It is found in the divine spirit of wholeness, and lies above the zone of material distortions and negations. It comes not supernaturally, but normally, through the immutable law of attraction. It is ever waiting for human souls to attune their own vibrations into unison with its own supernal harmonies. When the human consciousness becomes filled with truth, there is no room for error; and the latter, having no other abiding-place, becomes non-existent.

It is a hopeful sign of the times, that physics is becoming so refined and immaterial that it seems likely soon to dissolve into metaphysics.

In spite of the dark, ever-present shadow of materialism, there is great hope in the present attitude of institutional science. It is open to the logic of events as never before. It has been driven from its old earthworks, and is on the march, with destination undecided. Its present positions are tentative, its formulas are being recast, and its text-books, not yet a score of years old, are being relegated to basement storage.

As in ages past polytheism was displaced by monotheism, so now the great variety of separate and independent forces long recognized by science have been reduced to one infinite primal energy. The unity of all things, and their close interrelation, are felt and admitted. All that is pure in religion and true in science are converging towards each other. Whatever is natural is sacred, because it is permeated with the divine life. · Prophets and poets are becoming expert spiritual chemists, and the true constituents of the kingdom of heaven are scientifically recognized. The new dispensation will be ushered in, not with observation and external pomp, but silently, in its normal location, — the sanctuary of soul. Browning thus voices this sublime sentiment: —

> "But, friends,
> Truth is within ourselves: it takes no rise
> From outward things, whate'er you may believe.
> There is an inmost centre in us all,
> Where truth abides in fulness: and around
> Wall upon wall the gross flesh hems it in
> This perfect, clear perception — which is truth."

The chemistry of the future will include the scientific blending of spiritual and immaterial forces for definite ends: it will concern itself more with the internal, and less with the sensuous; more with cause, and less with effect. There will be an intelligent utilization of thought energy, and its values will be determined in the light of law. Just that nutrition and those ingredients that are able to satisfy the universal soul-hunger of humanity will be judiciously sought out, and their application intelligently provided for.

For ages the alchemist labored to discover some mysterious refining process through which the baser metals could be transmuted into gold. But modern science, with all its miracles, has failed to compass such a result. But a diviner and infinitely more valuable accomplishment has been realized. Scientific idealism is the expert alchemist whose invaluable services are freely at the command of every earnest soul. It can transmute the restless, chaotic forces of mankind into the golden harmony of human liberty and spiritual unfoldment.

There is a profusion of unmanifest health, strength, beauty, opulence, harmony, and courage waiting for appropriation. The higher unfoldment reveals the channel through which they may be assimilated, and the supply is endless.

The knowledge of the art of mental compounding is constantly expanding, so that with more consummate skill we work to purer ideals, and with more symmetrical models. Through positive formative thought we receive the title-deeds to invaluable possessions. With the wand of affirmation we project them into expression and actuality. The incarnation of truth is the transforming energy which rounds out and embellishes the soul-structure and its expressive physical instrument.

The ocean of life is boundless and shoreless, and we are consciously or unconsciously bathing in its crystalline waters. Vitality is pressing in upon us in the attempt to break through our false limitations.

The supernal chemistry which alone can combine those constituent elements which must mingle in order to the erection of normal human expression, is that which is divinely ordained through harmony with the One Mind or Oversoul. To vibrate in unison with the Universal Goodness introduces a consciousness of cosmic harmony.

The superficial and unintelligent belief in physical causation has been the racial stumbling-block, and nowhere has it been more pronounced than among the ranks of the devotees of so-called science. Keen institutional searchers peer into matter, expecting to discover its great secret through measures and tests. The laboratory methods of the modern physicist have so increased in delicacy, that through his psychological appliances, if he cannot actually weigh thought, he can at least determine its resulting intensity, volume, and continuity. Its intermittent energy may be tracked and followed among the brain-cells, but *it* ever eludes pursuit.

The "conservation of energy" has been for some time accepted as an ascertained fact, if not already axiomatic in modern science. Stated in common terms, this comprises the doctrine that though the forms and qualities of energy may change, nothing is ever added to or subtracted from the sum-total. So even the most ideal mental activity cannot create any *more* spiritual energy, but it may through recognition embody and express more of the existing universal.

The formative power contained in imaging thought, as exercised in accord with law, has not been gained, or even recognized, upon any level below that of highly developed humanity. As man comes into an intelligent understanding of his equipment of creative power, he will grasp the sceptre of his supersensuous sonship and kingship. So far as he had been "faithful over a few things," he will become "ruler over many." By faith he will be able to "remove mountains" of doubt and fear, and cast them into the sea of oblivion. Through a knowledge of the divine chemistry of being, he will subdue kingdoms and work righteousness.

We are sculptors, with tools in hand, sharp and keen; and around us is an endless quarry of unstained virgin marble, in which statues of beauty are confined, waiitng for us to emancipate them. By skilful touch we may awaken them into animated expression. Life is everywhere hidden away, ready to flow into the manifestation of the sons of God. Truth, immortal and invisible, is waiting to spring forth into expressive embodiment.

Paul had a glimpse of the transcendent power of its supernal spiritual chemistry when he declared, "All things are yours;" and he actually attempted their enumeration. How little have we grasped the import of such a scientific declaration! With the power of thought, the resolvent of love, and the transforming energy of truth, Paul's aphorism is interpreted to be, not an empty figure of speech, but a possible and practicable accomplishment. The inexhaustible fountain of power is the divinity within; and as our limitations are found to be entirely self-imposed, all barriers are swept away, and man leaps forward into the fulfilment of his divine destiny.

THE EDUCATION OF THOUGHT.

THOUGHT is the human motor. With the great majority, however, it exerts its force without definite aim or purpose. It is a building-power, but yet works to no plan or specification. Its operations may be compared to the work of a crazy carpenter, who, though always busy, nails up material at random. In the light of such experiences its real power and utility are unappreciated. Its forces, which, if properly directed, might be gigantic in accomplishment, are either misapplied or lapse into decadence.

The fact that, with law for a pilot, thought may take on supreme, yes, even divine potency, has not been grasped. The law-applying test is the great distinguishing feature of the present era. We are learning to look behind phenomena, and to trace the lines of sequence which have produced them. Just in proportion as we divine the *laws* of anything, we tame and harness it for service.

Electricity is as old as the material cosmos, but until now it has been useless from lack of lawful interpretation. The specific application of law was not attempted, because its universal reign has only recently come into recognition. It is indeed strange that the orderly energy of electricity should have so long remained undiscovered; but it is more unaccountable that the laws, powers, and uses of the ever-present thinking-faculty should have continued an unsolved problem. Thought is the grand fact and force in human existence, but yet no lesser force has been used so unintelligently. Most commonly it is like a boat floating upon shifting currents with oars and rudder unmanned. Its course is shaped and altered by every wind and tide, and its lading taken on in the same haphazard fashion.

There is nothing so much needed as thought-education in order that this ever-available force may perform the work for which it was designed in the human economy. A comprehension of its underlying laws is necessary to direct and utilize its great energy.

There is no lack of thought activity. This is pre-eminently a thinking age, keen, busy, and intense. Research goes *outward* in every possible direction. The illimitable cosmos is not too great, nor molecules or bacteria too small, to call forth its devoted pursuit. It exercises itself upon history, and delves among past events and civilizations, even though it finds only a grand panorama of human friction and limitation. Thought also centres itself upon the physical sciences; upon government, theology, ethics, and every other known subject except its *own* wonderful potency and utility. It is a busy mill; and into its ever-open hopper is poured a conglomerate grist, good, bad, and indifferent. It knows about everything but itself. Its food, though unlimited in quantity, is mainly of a negative, limited, and sensuous quality.

The grand office of thought is the upbuilding of a character or soul-structure which shall be symmetrical and substantial. It builds from within, and can find unlimited material in wholesome and perfect ideals. Educated thought educes or draws from the human divine centre the harmonious and the beautiful, and erects them into form and expression. Uneducated thought goes into the external for its material, and opens itself to that which is inharmonious and distorted. It incorporates all the limitations and false perceptions which conventionalism and traditionalism have made so plentiful, and its structure embodies their disorder and negation.

The thought of the *One Mind* is the eternal energy of the universe; and in proportion as human (or finited) thinking copies and traces its orderly laws, it takes on infinite vigor and usefulness. Humanity, through self-limitation, has closed itself against its divine heritage. Its lawful patrimony is *good* without any deviation. The thinking-power is the link whereby man may bind himself to what is eternal and immutable. As he grasps and holds the ideal he takes on its quality. The divine within him becomes him*self*. The "Word" which dwells in his inmost also becomes articulate, and is made flesh, or comes into externals.

Thought is not only the greatest but the only real power in the universe. Even on the mundane plane it shapes all external systems, governments, and institutions. Its subtle, silent waves dissolve dynasties, overturn empires, humanize animality, and inspire progress. Even though so generally misdirected, through its evolutionary undercurrents it is hastening forward the supremacy of truth in human consciousness.

Formerly only an occasional poet or prophet had visions of the higher reality, but now the uplifting power of positive thinking is becoming a grand and broadening inspiration. Previous to the recognition of universal law, thought energy was seemingly mystical and capricious, and its accomplishments were rated "supernatural." Now its mathematical and scientific precision is made clear. From dim and rare glances of its power and beauty, attainable only at intervals by gifted souls, it is becoming "matter of fact"— a practical every-day possession.

The world subjectively dwells among pictures of discord, disease, and self-limitation; but progressive volition will finally bring about a complete and universal rectification.

If the thought-craft has been floating at the mercy of every wind and tide, we must grasp the helm, man the oars, and begin to direct its course. The false thinking of the present — to some extent involuntary — comes from bad thinking-habits of the past. Like a meadow brook, it wears channels. Now is the time to begin to direct its course for the future. Lazy, careless, and morbid thought currents must give place to positive ideals, and these should be affirmed into actualization.

The only true ownership that we can gain of desirable "things" is through the medium of thought. In no other way can we make them truly *ours*. Title-deeds of material things are loose and weak compared with possession by ideals firmly held. We not only gain them, but actually make them *part of ourselves*.

If we have been missing the mark by careless and lawless thinking, let us begin the projection of right thought with earnestness and precision. Its power is gained from its intensity and continuity. With the vigorous use of these two pinions, its flight may be lofty, and unweighted by limitations. It will thus be able to gather and bring treasures into the storehouse of consciousness, and its rich fruitage will include all that is positive and divine. It is the force which verifies Paul's declaration: "All things [wholesome and perfect entities] are yours."

Men strive and toil for material wealth, but thought is a mint where coinage more valuable than gold is waiting for room to bestow itself. It will honor every draft that is made upon its treasury.

To link thought to the ideal transmutes it into the real and actual. Do we desire mental and physical harmony, holiness (wholeness), and everything else that is truly desirable? "Ask, and ye shall receive; seek, and ye shall find." The "finding" is the bringing into expression of the pure and the beautiful through the all-powerful instrumentality of intelligent concentration.

THE NATURE AND USES OF PAIN.

THE world has waged an unceasing warfare with pain. It has been regarded as the monster who despoils us of our pleasure, robs us of our repose, and whose dart is ever poised to strike us down. Its unwelcome presence has embittered every cup, and rendered life — otherwise so desirable — hardly worth the living. Sages and seers have occasionally divined its significance, but their interpretations have fallen upon deaf ears. Can it be possible that the vast majority of conventional judgments which have pronounced pain as a great adversary — evil and only evil — have been incorrect?

If the almost universal consensus of opinion has been at fault, how can such a widespread misapprehension be accounted for? Is the established order of nature wrong, or is the mistake in us, and in our point of view?

We shall assume that natural law, which is only another name for divine method, has not miscarried, and that in itself it is good, and only good. It, however, seems beneficent or baneful — to us — just according to our attitude toward it. Pain appears to be an enemy because of the common occupation of false standpoints which afford but a limited and distorted view of the human economy. They are mainly included in two great groups, which may be designated as those of materialistic science on the one hand, and traditional theological dogma on the other. Though greatly differing in other respects, they both regard man as a material being; that is, on this plane of development he is primarily and practically body. Much of the prevailing materialism is held unconsciously, but that fact does not mitigate its penalties.

But many intelligent observers would plausibly affirm that, from the standpoint of body, pain comes into the arena as a formidable and unrelenting antagonist. We shall try to show, however, that even such a statement is an error, or, at least, only a half truth. The body, as the normal, outward expression of man, is a co-operative adjunct, and not at cross purposes with him.

Materia medica, venerable with age, and eminently respectable, is one of the great departments of scientific materialism. It organizes its forces for the purpose of combating and obliterating pain, upon the theory that it is an intrinsic evil. An important subdivision of its agencies produces a partial paralysis of the sensory nerves, and thus destroys, not the cause of pain, but the perception of it. The patient wishes to be relieved of penalty, or, in other words, to have the link severed which binds effect to cause. It is possible to do this — temporarily or apparently — even though such "relief" may be a positive obstacle to a real cure. But if pain truly interpreted be only symptomatic, and not an evil *per se*, all logic and scientific method would indicate that treatment for its healing should be directed, not to itself, or even to its immediate occasion, but to underlying and primary causation.

Dogmatic theology, having recognized two great ubiquitous principles in the world, known as good and evil, closely matched and each striving for the mastery, enthrones Pain as a Prince among hostile forces. It is reputed to be one of the results of "the Fall;" but it may be incidentally suggested that if that event were regarded as subjective, instead of objective and historic, it would have a deep element of truth. It is, however, made to appear that God sends pain without any good reason, and even when uninvited by man. How and why the Infinite Goodness should do this has always been an unsolvable problem to theology. It has been either a great "mystery," or else relegated in its origin to the action of the "Prince of Evil." Many well-meaning and conscientious souls regard it as a "visitation of Providence" — an evil, but yet in some way necessary, and to be heroically endured. They look upon it as belonging to the established human economy — in its "fallen estate."

Discomfort, therefore, instead of being an educational negative or background, is, to human consciousness, made to appear as a positive entity. With suffering uninterpreted or misinterpreted, seeming adverse forces become so overwhelming that many are driven into pessimism and atheism. The universe becomes a seeming contradiction or a riddle. Law, or the operation of the cosmic order, appears implacably hostile; and humanity is bruised and broken in the grind of its ponderous machinery. The earth is filled with sighs, groans, and tears, as the consequence of such an unequal and hopeless contest.

But pain, so deep and universal in its phenomena, must possess a meaning of vital import to mankind. To judge it superficially is an error of such proportion that it distorts — to our view — the whole human economy.

We have habitually looked upon the divine, primal energy, in its operations upon man, as coming from without instead of from within. If suffering breaks in arbitrarily from the outside, whether from the Deity or any lesser source, we may well despair. In the attempt to solve its problems, the materialist is logically forced to agnosticism, or worse; and the theologian only succeeds in extenuating its fierceness by the assumption that after the event called death an abnormal amount of happiness will be bestowed in the nature of a compensation.

Having noted some of the aspects of pain as it

appears from an average sensuous standpoint, we may advance toward a truer estimate. It always indicates life. Its sharpest pangs tell of a keen sensibility, and an intense, vital working-force, which is striving to correct our mistakes and straighten our crookedness. It is a developer, refiner, and polisher. With all its scowling features, it is more friendly to us than we, through ignorance, are to ourselves. Its horrors are only the friction produced by the quick rush of divine, vital energy to do its wholesome and purifying work. It is ever hurrying on to transform our disorder into order, and friction is thereby excited.

Disease is a disturbance, incited by a supreme effort of the intrinsic man to express himself through an external and grosser medium which is yet lagging behind. A fever is a quickened and desperate struggle of the immaterial self to expel and overcome obstructions in its instrument of manifestation. When accomplished, the outward medium is clearer and purer. Is, then, the fever a good thing? Abstractly and ideally, no; provisionally, useful just at the time it appears, because it never comes unnecessarily.

Disease, of whatever name, signifies the lack of ease, rather than a thing in itself. It is the designation of a negative condition, and not of a positive or divinely created entity. It is always simply a deficiency, even though appearing with differentiated external phenomena, which have been dignified and made realistic and "scientific" by formal diagnosis and classification.

Mental and physical pangs are one and the same. The distinction is only that of the plane upon which the inner lack, or misplacement, most prominently expresses itself. It either has, or has not yet, reached out into the ultimates of the material organism.

The body, while no part of the real man, is an outward index of the quality of his consciousness. The qualitative expression, however, comes so gradually that the interrelation of the two is generally overlooked. The original source of pain is always mental. It comes from the abuse, or misplacement, of the thought forces, which in themselves are good, and the result is disorder.

We conventionally attribute our physical ills to the influence of the weather, water, air, climate, dampness, work, cold, draughts, malaria, bacteria, and contagion. Granted all these may be occasions, but the primary cause lies deeper. We hunt for a "scapegoat" outside, and if none can be conveniently found we make one. Human pride contrives to shift the responsibility; that is, from its own standpoint. But unless receptivity carelessly opens the door, external negatives do not find an entrance. Subjective incubation must precede overt manifestation.

The thinking-faculty, with its untiring imagining power, is the active agent which gives tone and color to all human expression; and, if unregulated, it invites pain, which at length puts in a corrective appearance. The invitation may be given unconsciously; but the reprover never comes unbidden, and never until its presence is reformatory. Its mission is educational, but we are averse to its teaching.

The established order in itself is harmonious, and all human infelicity comes from non-conformity. This postulate receives abundant indorsement from universal analogy and experience, when they are intelligently interpreted. The clear understanding of this grand principle, of itself tends directly to palliate the bitterness of our distresses, and measurably to overcome them. The belief that the "courses of nature" are unfriendly to man adds a crushing weight to the seeming burden of human ills. But when, through the discipline of penalty, he is turned about, and brought into conformity with law, judgment is satisfied. True, its reformatory work may be gradual, but none the less certain. Correction, even though so universally misconstrued, is only the executive force of *Love*. All phenomena of the divine economy, which include the human, have positive use and purpose.

We are therefore led to recognize pain in every possible guise as negatively good, though never ideally excellent or desirable. Its thorough cure comes only from an intelligent correction of its primal cause. Even though it present a drawn sword, it is really a guardian angel to turn us away from the sensuous Eden of ignorance. But for such protection we should go on burning and bruising our bodies and indulging our appetites and passions to the length of self-destruction. We are well aware that "a burnt child dreads the fire," but have failed logically to carry forward such an educational method, in its application to deeper negatives like neuralgia, rheumatism, and fever. Such corrective conditions have been regarded as calamities, coming in some unexplained way, or as "visitations of Providence" that we would obliterate in order to escape from their physical sensations.

It is true that some progress has been made, so that physical distresses are often traced to violations of hygienic law, and the "visitation" hypothesis is becoming somewhat obsolete. The observance of objective sanitation is a step in advance, but far from a final one. Its limit of progress is confined to a narrow range, so long as man fails to study himself, and gives all his attention and research to things outside. He investigates the laws of everything, except the one thing most important — his own constitution. He carries his pursuit of hygienic science so far that he almost unconsciously falls into a worse bondage than that of the former state, when he regarded Providence or chance as the source of his woes. The deeper he peers into the complexity of external "laws of health," the more hoplessly involved does he become.

But the limitations that we have set up — or, rather, that the race in general has imposed — must be gradually moved along, rather than at once pulled down. Until subjective quarantine has been intelligently erected, that which is objective cannot be entirely disregarded. So long as our own doors are open to foes from without, we will be obliged to meet them at a great disadvantage in the fields outside.

All pain is mental; but we designate that part physical which has ultimated itself into the external degree. The inner mind or life is constantly trying to remove obstructions and cast out intruders. It is a light striving to penetrate a dull, murky medium. The discomfort and inflammation which result from a sliver in the finger come not from the sliver, but from the effort to cast out the intruder. The principle is still more evident with pains of a general or interior character.

From the premises and conclusions already noted, and others which cannot be presented in a brief paper, we are led to affirm both the rationality and scientific adaptability of metaphysics for the healing of human disease, upon whatever plane manifested. However, owing to ages of self-imposed limitation, we cannot at once assert complete material emancipation, but may easily discover the road which leads toward the goal, and press on in that direction.

The host of external things which we and our ancestors have dreaded, expected, taken for granted, and bowed the knee to, cannot immediately be subdued; but as we grow in the understanding of mental and spiritual law, and its application, they may be gradually transmuted from reigning despots into docile servitors.

Physical discomforts are the sequential attendants of so-called physical transgressions; but never has one appeared that did not have its ultimate source in negative mental conditions. Erroneous thinking is always back of violated physical hygiene. The overt suffering only expresses that which has been previously installed and made subjectively at home. If the fountain be pure, such purity will gradually extend to physical ultimates, and the reverse holds equally true.

When Paul in his letter to the Philippians enumerated things that are "true," "honorable," "just," "pure," "lovely," and "of good report," as being profitable to think upon, he wrote not only as the apostle of a living faith, but as a metaphysician having a scientific understanding of the laws of the mental constitution of man. If we would render a visit of the Pain-Missionary unnecessary, we must take the helm of the thought-craft and intelligently direct its course. If we have been floating among rubbish, we must man the oars and pull for clear water. The sensitive, living consciousness must be steered away from the shoals of inharmonies, negatives, and forebodings, into the invigorating deeps of a positive spiritual optimism.

As ideals and affirmations of wholeness, purity, strength, and spirituality are held with a firm grasp, despair, disease, and a host of other related negative beliefs, are displaced; and when they depart they take all their train of possible pain-sequences with them. Whatever is internal and immaterial is always reaching out to embody itself; and this law is universal.

If the ego has been dwelling in the basement of its nature, where the furnishings are sensual, disorderly, and pessimistic, and where the atmosphere is heavy with abnormity, the pain-messenger comes with his goads to drive the consciousness higher. But it would never disturb us if we would go of our own choice. Its visit is that of an Angel of Light, even though outwardly disguised, to save us from ourselves and our self-made spectres. No enemy, other than those harbored within, from any possible realm can harm us.

"A man's foes shall be they of his own household." His invited guests, in the shape of his own morbid thoughts, at length turn traitors. The character of his mental picture-gallery determines the tone of his living subjective world, and sooner or later the objective universe dissolves into vibratory correspondence. To our consciousness this law is slow in its fruition — often so slow that we are unaware of its operation; but the legislation of the "Medes and Persians" was not surer.

The world tries to parry pain, but refuses to learn its merciful lesson. The sensualist would fain dismiss it, but it guards his true and deeper selfhood from his false and mistaken personality. Through a humane but misunderstood discipline he finally "comes to himself," or to a consciousness of his real Being. He clings to the Egypt of physical sensation until he is forcibly driven out from its degrading servitude.

Pain is a saviour; for without its divine redemption sin would increase until it fruited in spiritual death. In so far as *materia medica* drowns its voice, and paralyzes or intercepts its benignant messages, it tends to degrade man toward the animal plane of mere physical sensation. Only by overcoming and rising above the control of a sense-consciousness can he attain to his true ideal, — a "living soul." The inner Christ draws upward; but the "old man" struggles, resists, and beseeches to be let alone. But the Divine Law will continue its educational and evolutionary work until material limitations are finally outgrown.

THE SUB-CONSCIOUS MIND.

EVERY unit is made up of unlike elements. The mentality of each individual, therefore, though a unified entity, contains factors which are quite dissimilar in their offices and modes of operation. It is only through an intelligent discrimination of these various phases of mental activity that phenomena can be correctly resolved and their *modus operandi* discerned and utilized.

In the present brief study of the sub-conscious realm, it is not proposed to dwell upon its more speculative and technical aspects, but rather to note a few evident tendencies and sequences which are of practical import.

Any radical misapprehension of the normal relations of the great silent or submerged mentality to its more active counterpart must be fraught with serious results to human welfare and progress.

The realm in question is largely an unknown one, having been yet but scantily explored. A better appreciation of its scope, control, and use is most desirable, not only to students of psychology, but to every human being.

But the views of psychologists are quite unlike.

Some give this department little attention, while others broaden its range to cover nearly all phenomena. By some writers the two phases or different activities of mind are termed the objective and subjective, but we suggest that conscious and sub-conscious seem more fitting.

In attempting to define concisely what we believe to be the functions of the submerged mentality, we may first negatively suggest that, though in close connection, it is by no means identical with the intuitive faculty. The latter — often called the spiritual perception — is that clear-cut vision which the developed ego possesses to discern truth at sight, or without the employment of a logical process. It is a quick discerner of the grade and value of principles and things, and by exact measurement is able to gauge and compare them with the normal Universal Good. None are without it; but with the great majority it is yet only rudimentary. It is the supremest sense belonging to humanity, while both the conscious and sub-conscious domains are included in the changeable and growing personality. The sub-conscious mind, therefore, while hidden, is quite differentiated from the spiritual or divine selfhood. It is rather a growing storehouse or depository of thought, emotion, and every-day experience. It is susceptible to discipline and improvement, in proportion as the laws of its operation are understood. It is a kind of sum-total of past states of consciousness, laid away, but not lost. Like any other accumulation of slow growth, its quality is only subject to gradual change. In many respects it seems like an independent personality. It reasons, hopes, fears, loves, hates, and wills all below the surface of conscious mind, the latter being often entirely unaware of its operations and conclusions.

Another most important fact: It acts automatically upon the physical organism. It cognizes external facts, conditions, limitations, and even contagions, quite independent of its active counterpart. One may, therefore, "take" a disease and be unaware of any exposure. The sub-consciousness has been unwittingly trained to fear, accept, and expect it; and it is this quality, rather than the mere inert matter of the body, that succumbs. Matter is never the actor, but always acted upon.

If we look upon a lake, we see only that insignificant portion which is upon the surface. Below is perhaps ninety-nine hundredths of its volume, beyond observation. In like manner the sub-conscious mentality contains layer upon layer, and deep below deep. As occasion offers, memory is able to plunge in and bring some things to the surface; but these, all included, comprise but a mere fraction of the contents of this great hidden storehouse. On rare occasions, however, some great emergency — perhaps most often observed in a drowning experience —

draws back the sub-conscious curtain, and the ego gains a quick panoramic view of the thoughts and transactions of a lifetime. This phenomenon, though rare, is exceedingly significant. It proves that no mental picture, or even thought, has been obliterated. They are only temporarily out of sight.

As before noted, this silent mental partner, in operation seems to be a living, thinking personality, conducting affairs on his own account. It is a compound of almost unimaginable variety, including wisdom and foolishness, logic and nonsense, and yet having a working unitary economy. It is a hidden force to be dealt with and educated, for it is often found insubordinate and unruly. It refuses co-operation with its lesser but more active and wiser counterpart. It is very "set" in its views, and only changes its quality and opinions by slow degrees. But, like a pair of horses, not until these two mental factors can be trained to pull together can there be harmony and efficiency.

The submerged personality may be compared to a reservoir, or cistern, into which there is constantly flowing a small stream of conscious thinking. If the mass be turbid, it is to be inferred that the past inflow has been of that prevailing quality. Only a changed influx can gradually reform its character. No thought is lost. Each mental creation not only goes out in objective vibrations, but also registers itself in its subjective repository. As in a chemical combination, each ingredient adds something of its own quality and shading.

In the light of these principles, what a tremendous responsibility is involved in every action of the creative imaging faculty! Nothing has been so lightly regarded as a thought, and yet objectively we are thinking to the world, and subjectively into an indestructible habitation of our own. The "every idle word," for which men shall be judged, when rightly interpreted, is a scientific statement, but the judgment is inherent and continuous. But sequential penalty is not less serious than that which has been supposed to be arbitrary.

The immense utility of auto-suggestion is seen in the intelligent exercise of the conscious mentality in projecting instalments of its quality into the sub-conscious domain. This is a process through which every wholesome and grand ideal, mental and physical, may not only be accumulated, but put upon compound interest. Additions may be made to the capital stock "in season and out of season," for the law is immutable. Even to think good thoughts mechanically is excellent, for the process soon grows to be spontaneous, and thereby a most vital creative mental habit is formed.

The cumulative energy and quality of the sub-consciousness, while automatically exact, is almost universally unappreciated. To lay one brick or set one stone is not to build a house; but continue the process with intelligent design, and at length the structure towers up in beautiful proportion. With scientific exactitude one may make himself what he will, by thinking his thoughts into the right form, and continuing the process until they solidify. But careless and lawless thinking sets in motion forces which pull in opposite directions, and rending and confusion are the result.

The thought material which is created for deposit should always be better and higher than that of past attainment and accumulation. The power of accomplishment is thereby invigorated and increased. The supernal aim should be, receptivity to the Universal Spirit of Wholeness (theologically called the Holy Spirit), and this has a positive transforming influence.

The intellect, will, memory, and even the physical organism, gradually articulate the pent-up forces of the inner realm. Thus the "Word is made flesh" by coming into ultimation and visibility.

THE PSYCHOLOGY OF CRIME.

EVERY outward manifestation is a harvest. No full-fledged or overt act takes place that is not the lawful sequence of previous incubation, nourishment, and growth. When a criminal offence "happens," the usual concern is only with the event, its details, and the adequate punishment of the offender. The act is vividly outlined, its heinous features are analyzed, the guilt of its supposed author is passed upon, and a demand is made for the enforcement of the proper penalty. This comprises all that society feels called upon to do in the premises. A blow has been dealt to the community in one of its parts, and the community deals a proportionate one in return; and thus the transaction is closed, and the books balanced. Possibly some "motive" may be discovered, which forms the last or immediate step behind the act; but farther back, or in broader scope, neither general nor special investigation is thought necessary.

While deeper research may not be practicable officially, it is of great importance that there should be a more general and intelligent appreciation of the processes through which crime and disorder are generated. The superficial and objective spirit of our Western civilization is unfavorable for a thorough study of primary and subjective causation. The Within that finds expression in the Without lies hidden away from the popular gaze, and only through some application of psychological law can it be clearly interpreted.

No criminal motive ever grows in weight so that it finally preponderates, except by slow and intangible accretions. However spontaneous or impulsive any given offence may appear in its method, the foundation upon which it rears itself has been slowly formed from a variety of sediment. The great lesson of modern science is that nothing " happens." Everything that comes is pushed from behind. This philosophy, which is accepted by all careful thinkers, and perhaps theoretically by a wider circle, is yet far from being acknowledged as a practical truism. We live under an economy of law absolutely universal in its scope; but while no link in the chain of detail includes the least element of chance, there is no fatalism involved in this perfect order. On the contrary, all real freedom comes only from its aid, and through intelligent conformity. Law is always in readiness to serve us; but we must adopt its methods.

There is no pessimism involved in a study of the generation of crime; for the very laws and forces which by abnormal use bring it into expression are abundantly potent, when rightly used, for the production of its normal and wholesome opposites. While recognizing an upward trend as broad as humanity, and an optimism which views "evil" only as a subjective condition, yet it is evident that there are operative at the present time special forces that directly germinate crime and disorder. It is said that about seven thousand murders have taken place within the limits of the United States during the last year, and offences of lesser degree have been so numerous that even an approximate estimate can hardly be formed. However, we are dealing not with statistics but principles.

The luxury and artificialism of our modern civilization, the struggle for wealth and social position, the pursuit of sensuous gratification — are powerful factors which disintegrate character, obscure high ideals, and bring disorder and abnormity into overt manifestation. But perhaps a more potent element of demoralization than any of these is found in the deluge of delineated criminality and other morbid reading-matter, in which the community mentally dwells, and the malaria of which it is constantly inhaling. This great, unceasing supply of unsound mental pabulum comes in the forms of offensive sensationalism in the daily press, flashy illustrated weeklies, and the cheap "blood and thunder" fiction which is devoured in unlimited quantities by youthful and immature minds.

That a large ratio of space in the great dailies is crowded with matter that in varying degree may be classed as abnormal and unwholesome is a palpable and unquestioned fact. It is also quite unnecessary to prove the existence of the flashy illustrated weeklies. Their numbers and suggestiveness are evidenced by the gaping crowd always seen gathered about the news-shop windows, gazing at pictorial representations which are as near the border-line of indecency as it is possible to be and escape the law. The world is full of "suggestion" of every quality. That which is distinctively classed as "hypnotic" is in quantity but "a drop in the bucket" when compared with the every-day variety.

The sediment which settles from all these turbid agitations furnishes the soil out of which murders, suicides, sexual immoralities, thefts, and numberless other disorders are the continual growth and fruitage. If unsound meat or decayed vegetables are palmed off upon the public, the guilty offender is arrested and punished; but youthful and pure consciousness may be invaded and poisoned, and all is taken as a matter of course. Society concerns itself considerably with the punishment of crime, but very little with its prevention. The penalty for overt criminality is conventionally supposed to act as a powerful deterrent; but it has only a limited power in that direction. While government — or organized society — cannot take legal cognizance of anything less than overt acts, it is important that there should be a general and intelligent knowledge of the constructive process through which criminals are made. They do not come by chance, but grow; and their growth is through suggestion. The immediate psychical impulse which precedes the overt act is but one link in a chain which reaches back indefinitely.

Society in general is responsible for its criminality. Its criminals are not detached units on the outside, but rather eruptions from within. The circulation of the body politic is impure. Prevailing morbid thoughts and ideas naturally find embodiment, an illustrative specimen of which was seen in Guiteau, the slayer of President Garfield. As well cut off an occasional thistle-head, with the expectation of killing the crop, as hope to exterminate crime through the deterrent power of legislative penalty.

The lack of moral and social progress is due to a prevailing sensuous superficiality, which concerns itself only with phenomena instead of deep causative forces. Criminality is purely expressive and symptomatic. The laws of mind are unswerving and exact. Mental conditions, including all qualities of thought and suggestion, tend to outward expression. To illustrate: An atrocious murder takes place. The daily press, by full detail and embellishments, graphically engraves it, with all its suggestiveness, upon the public consciousness. Its passion and abnormity are held up and analyzed until they permeate the whole psychic atmosphere. The criminal is surrounded by the halo of romance and glamour of notoriety. His likeness is given a prominent place in a leading column, and is thus brought before the eyes of unnumbered thousands. And recently modern "enterprise" reproduces the whole scene, through cuts or engravings, not omitting the weapons. A mental picture of the *tout ensemble* is thus photographed upon all minds and memories. The details are read, re-read, and discussed. Where there is any mind containing, in some degree, a chord of savagery, animalism, or morbidity, it is stirred into corresponding vibration. Possibly some, who have been near the verge of a similar act, are pushed over the line. But no one escapes untarnished. The soundest and sanest minds cannot thus have the imaging faculty tampered with, without some deterioration, even though it be unconscious.

In the evolutionary transition from primeval or animal man to humanity, there has been brought over a large residuum of animality, and this forms a kind of false self, which is stirred and stimulated by outward morbid suggestion. A pugilistic encounter, a street-fight, or even a dog-fight, will, as if by magic, draw a crowd, much as a magnet will gather iron filings. In many cases a man seems to be but a thin veneer to the animal within, the latter often breaking through from outside suggestion. The occasional boy who starts out with hatchet and pistol to rob, or fight with Indians, as suggested by mental pictures drawn from the great juvenile library of "blood and thunder" fiction, only goes somewhat farther in the same direction than all other boys travel who live upon the same mental stimulant.

A recent notable murder and trial furnished a striking illustration of the extent to which a single tragic event can fill the public mind and consciousness. The official trial of the accused party was but little more exhaustive than thousands of unofficial trials which took place in drawing-rooms and business offices. But this is by no means solely the fault of publishers and editors. The public taste needs to be rectified. Every one who reads, dwells upon, and rehearses such a quality of thought is in some measure responsible. All this is common, not because of any intention to give currency to that which is unwholesome, but from a lack of knowledge of psychological laws and the power of suggestion. A true understanding of mental philosophy is all that is needed. As soon as we intelligently grasp the laws of any force or thing, we have it not only under control, but harnessed for use. The principles of suggestion, like edged tools, when rightly used, are of wonderful utility. Its power to project high ideals is unlimited, but it recoils when misdirected.

The modern "daily" possesses a gigantic power to mould and color public consciousness; and its conduct involves a very grave responsibility, which its man-

agers either lightly regard, or are quite unaware of;
but, after all, it is but an articulation of that which
preponderates in human thought. A majority *want*
sensationalism, and supply always responds to demand.
But if rapid money-making could be made
secondary, the daily press would be an immense educational
and uplifting force in society. In general
observations, it would be unjust to intimate that all
papers are on the same plane, for there are all grades
and qualities. Principles only are here considered,
and when once understood they will make their own
application discriminately. The purveyors of the
daily press cannot be expected to be disinterested
philanthropists, more than other men, though their
power is gigantic and their responsibility peculiar.
As things are, the main hope for reform must begin
with the public, or on the side of demand. The great
need is a more intelligent understanding of the psychological
laws of suggestion and subjective realism
as causative forces. Results can only be modified
through internal and underlying antecedents, and not
by mere external repression.

The mechanical and news-gathering facilities of a
great modern daily are marvellous. It is comparatively
a new and unprecedented force, for no former
period can be compared with it. But, gentlemen of
the daily press, why is it that under the plea of
" enterprise " or giving " the news," a murder in California,
a robbery in Arkansas, or some nameless out-

rage in Alabama, should be put in thought pictures, framed, and hung up in the mental chambers of millions, where high ideals are scarce for lack of room? Why should the horrors of lynchings, the morbidity of suicides, or even the details of catastrophes, be branded upon thousands of sensitive souls, where their scars will be indelible? A material photograph may be destroyed in an instant, while an immaterial one, printed by the imaging faculty, may remain for a life-time, often forcing its way into the consciousness uncalled for, or even when forbidden.

When the wise man uttered the familiar aphorism, "As a man thinketh in his heart, so is he," he expressed not merely a moral maxim, but a scientific truism. What men mentally dwell upon they become or grow like. Thought, even when centred upon a non-entity, in proportion to its intensity and continuity confers subjective realism. Not by chance, but by law, each mental delineation leaves its distinctive hue in the grand composite which makes up character. The undisciplined thinking-faculty has a sponge-like absorbability of the medium which surrounds it, and only by systematic idealism can it be trained to close its avenues against discordant and depressing environment. Thought projected in specific directions soon forms its own channels, which are rapidly deepened by habit. When turned upon the pure, the true, and the beautiful, these positives soon cast out their negative opposites.

The quality of thinking determines consciousness, and consciousness forms character. Character is, therefore, nothing more nor less than an habitual quality of consciousness. It is often supposed to consist of action, but it is that which is back of action. Any demoralization which comes from without does not come direct, but from the sympathetic vibration of corresponding unisons within. Action is often temporarily modified from motives of outward policy, but its constant effort is to become a true copy of the inner pattern.

The scientific way to destroy evil is not to hold it up and analyze it in order to make it hateful, but rather to put it out of the consciousness. To the degree that one does not see it, to him it becomes non-existent, because there is nothing to arouse its vibrations within. But it is important to remember that evil is real only as a subjective condition.

Whether or not we so wish, we are modified by every picture thrown upon the mental canvas. No matter to what extent one may detest a crime, he cannot immerse his consciousness in its turbid waves without taking on some of its slime and sediment.

But outside of what is distinctively classed as crime, the outpicturing of everything of a negative or inharmonious nature is unprofitable. The frictions, accidents, discords, and every other lack of harmony, of whatever name, occupy room in the consciousness which is of value. A thousand objective normal human developments attract no attention, while the single abnormity is put in the lens and thrown upon the screen. Its kind is thereby propagated. Occasional "outs" are made so important that they almost appear to be the rule. Reform will come only so fast as the necessity for more ideal mental pictures is appreciated. All real entities were formed by the Creator, and all are good; so that the abnormal when displaced from the human consciousness finds no resting-place.

The real world we dwell in is our thought world, rather than the material objects which surround us. The color of all outward environment depends upon the glasses through which we view it. The human consciousness is like an endless corridor in a picture gallery, each visitor executing and hanging his own works of art. His preference is determined by the character of those before which he lingers.

THE SIGNS OF THE TIMES.

A NEW light is dawning upon the human horizon. Its golden beams are penetrating into the damp, dark caverns of pessimistic realism, and transforming them into the abodes of spiritual brightness and optimism. The divinity of man — so long in eclipse that it has seemed well nigh lost — is manifestly asserting itself, and indications are not wanting that it is soon to find normal and rightful dominance.

There is an unprecedented condition of fluidity among general conventions in religion, science, ethics, and, in fact, the whole philosophy of life and being. The very fact that opinions, systems, theories, and doctrines were never before so fluidized, is a positive indication that everything will all the more easily rise or fall to the point of its own specific gravity.

A formal, dogmatic, and ceremonial Christianity is giving place to vital spiritual unfoldment that is befitting to man's constitution and being. Faith is newly defined. It is brought from the realm of the dim, distant, and uncertain future, into present reality and positive manifestation. The soul-hunger of humanity is being newly diagnosed, and its satisfaction definitely and intelligently provided for.

There is so much to encourage seekers after truth, that each one should strive, not only to broaden his own horizon, but also to lead his brothers and sisters to higher and more inspiring outlooks. Having in the past regarded inspiration as finished and complete, men have been willing to supinely rest in conditions, mistakenly supposed to be normal, holding in view only some detached fragment of the great rounded Unity of Truth. Like the bone of an animal, or the branch of a tree, such fractional aspects are not only meaningless, but misleading, when out of general relation.

The powers, uses, and possibilities of the human mind, under new interpretations, comprise a new Revelation. It is incomparably more wonderful than the most extravagant accomplishments, and even dreams, of material progress.

For ages men have crowded their energies in the pursuit of new physical and intellectual achievements, anticipating that human satisfaction and felicity were to be found along these lines, if they were persistently followed. But they were mistaken. The spiritual motor of scientific idealism is transcendently greater in potency than if the material dreams had all been actualized.

But an earthy and sensuous realism will only yield the ground inch by inch; and there will be "wars and rumors of wars," and other active manifestations of animalism, before the human consciousness is generally developed upon the higher planes. The wonderful significance of the GREAT TRANSITION is yet but faintly imagined, but TRUTH is invincible. In the great upheavals of the present era, nothing that is real in religion, science, or humanity will be destroyed. But the false, the unreal, and the external will be sloughed off. Arrested development will only increase retributive friction.

The established order, which is Good, and which is anchored in Good, will forever remain unshaken. Man is "feeling after" and finding God, both within and around him. Divine revelations, no longer confined to one narrow channel, are being sought after and found in all directions. The more deeply that physical science penetrates in its studies of all phenomena, the more nearly does it come to the divine and spiritual basis of all things.

The rosy dawn of a new and higher evolutionary dispensation already welcomes the eyes of those who occupy the more elevated standpoints. The potential "kingdom of heaven" is within man. As this great truth brightens in human consciousness, there will be a general emancipation from all low and limited conditions.

Such an IDEAL is to be held firmly in view until it comes into full actualization.

www.ingramcontent.com/pod-product-compliance
Lightning Source LLC
Chambersburg PA
CBHW020645230426
43665CB00008B/324